NATURAL DISCIPLESHIP

NATURAL DISCIPLESHIP

STEVE HARRIS

SET FREE

CONTENTS

CHAPTER 1

INTRODUCTION

Are you experiencing your highest fulfillment and purpose in life? Jesus said, "I came that they may have life and have it abundantly." (John 10:10). Our highest fulfillment and potential will come by becoming and experiencing all that God created us to be. Jesus made it very clear that our deepest joy will come from becoming growing, multiplying disciples of Christ.

If you owned a manufacturing company, and your product was smartphones, and you went to the end of the assembly line, and you did not see smartphones coming off, you would be in some other business. We need a prototype of what a disciple should look like.

Jesus gave us the description of a disciple when he called Peter and Andrew to be his disciples. He said in Matthew 4:19, "Follow me, and I will make you fishers of men." "Follow" is relational. "Make" is transformational. "Fisher" is missional. A disciple is someone who is following Christ, who is being changed by Christ, and who is committed to the mission of Christ.

Do you have the resources you need to grow as a follower of Christ, to lead those outside the faith to Christ, and to help them grow to also become multiplying followers of Christ? There is a great need for Christian ministry resources that will equip followers of Christ to share their faith and make disciples in a natural, relational, conversational, and personal way.

RELATIONAL MINISTRY

We need to present the gospel in the context of trusted relationships. Many people come to Christ over a long period of time, needing multiple meetings as opposed to a quick fifteen-minute presentation to close the deal. We need to start at the beginning of what it means to be created in God's image, rather than the fact that all have sinned and are separated from God.

The problem with the concept of relationship evangelism is that it often becomes an excuse for no evangelism. In any relationship, there comes a time when we must take initiative to engage people with an invitation to discuss spiritual things.

So, what about an approach to evangelism and discipleship that will include your story, my story, and God's story in a conversational, natural way?

THE MOST EFFECTIVE EVANGELISM AND DISCIPLESHIP

Personal spiritual conversations provide the most effective method of evangelism and discipleship today. It says in Proverbs 20:5, "The purpose in a man's heart is like deep water, but a man of understanding will draw it out." This can only happen by asking good questions to draw out what is in their heart.

The Apostle John understood the limitations of certain kinds of communication. He told his readers in 2 John 12, "Though I have much to write to you, I would rather not use paper and ink. Instead, I hope to come to you and talk face to face, so that our joy may be complete." John understood that the best kind of communication is face-to-face. People need "face time."

Jesus spent three and a half years pouring into twelve men, but he gave even more attention to the inner circle of Peter, James, and John. He had an even deeper relationship with John as "the disciple whom Jesus loved. "

PRESENTATION OR CONVERSATION?

Many evangelism and discipleship plans are primarily an approach that is a presentation rather than a conversation. With the fresh needs of a new generation in mind, NATURAL DISCIPLESHIP has been developed. This approach is relationally driven, respectful of each person's value and worth as an individual, and yet it is intentional, sequential, and practical. You will be exposed to a series of Bible discussions that are filled with relational, open-ended questions, and yet focused on God's word as the reference. **All questions will be set off in bold text** to highlight where you should stop and discuss the material from a personal perspective. The leader or the coach can read a few paragraphs and then ask the student to read a few paragraphs. Both of them can alternate reading until they come to a question, and then both can answer.

THE PROBLEM

Jesus gave us one clear commission before He ascended to heaven. Make disciples. That's it. Many churches today are simply not getting the job done. Over 85% of church attenders will tell you they have never been discipled by anyone. All of the polls are indicating that people who claim to be Christians do not have lives that are significantly different from secular people. If worship services and small groups were getting the job done, we would be seeing a much higher caliber of believer than we see today.

THE SOLUTION

Personal evangelism and discipleship is the foundation for making disciples. The one-on-one or one-on-two connection is the only place we find significant accountability. A person can attend a small group and still not be held accountable for their growth. Personal evangelism and discipleship are the most effective ways to fulfill the Great Commission. We desperately need great worship services and small groups, but we also need personal accountability as a foundation for making strong reproducing disciple-makers.

THE SECRET: MULTIPLICATION RATHER THAN ADDITION

If you were an incredibly gifted evangelist and God used you to lead 3,000 people a day to Christ, you would have a very successful ministry according to any standards. But if the world's population did not increase, it would still take you 5,000 years to win the whole world to Christ. But what if you won just one person to Christ and spent a full year helping them get rooted and grounded in the faith through NATURAL DISCIPLESHIP? Then you trained them with transferable concepts that they could use with someone else, and they took the next year to do the same thing as you discipled someone else. Through multiplication, you could win and disciple over 1,000 people in ten years, and it would be mathematically possible to reach the population of the whole world in 35 years.

WHAT ABOUT YOU?

Are you investing in addition or multiplication?

Paul said this to his disciple Timothy, "and what you have heard from me in the presence of many witnesses entrust to faithful men, who will be able to teach others also." (2 Timothy 2:2)

This is a description of four generations of disciples, starting with Paul, who taught Timothy, who would teach faithful men who would be equipped to teach others. This is the power of multiplication. The key to this is transferable concepts that can be handed down from one generation of disciples to the next.

NATURAL DISCIPLESHIP is a systematic, sequential approach to relationship evangelism and discipleship that is quickly transferable from one person to the next.

The impact of this approach to making disciples is that it may be taught and caught as you are going through your busy, daily life, using face-to-face meetings and culturally relevant instruction.

Note: The English Standard Version (ESV) translation was used for bible citations in this document unless noted.

CHAPTER 2

OVERVIEW

Natural Discipleship is a simple nine-step process to equip the body of Christ to reach the people in their network of relationships with the gospel of Christ and train them to become multiplying disciples of Christ.

1 Sharing His Story: There are a thousand different kinds of gospel tracts available for people to use in sharing the gospel, so why is there a need for another one? Most gospel tracts are a presentation with no opportunity for dialogue. Steps to Knowing God is not a monologue; it is a dialogue. This is a guided discussion in which every point of the gospel is followed by a discussion question designed to hear the heart of the person receiving the gospel.

2 Deeper Study of the Gospel—Life's Most Important Questions: This is a thorough discussion of the gospel, which capitalizes on the deepest questions everyone is asking.

1. Where did I come from?
2. Who am I?
3. Why am I here?
4. Where am I going?

It is a guided, sequential, relational discussion of your story, my story, and God's story. As the participants read together, they will come to many questions that will move them into a natural sharing of their spiritual values and a discovery of the power of the gospel.

3 Initial Studies for New Believers—The Groundwork Series: Every follower of Christ needs to be rooted and grounded in the faith. This discussion guide for new believers and those who have never received a strong foundation is a six-part study of some essential truths for followers of Christ. In the same format of "your story, my story and God's story", the participants will discover the most fundamental, crucial, and indispensable truths for the Christian life.

4 Inductive Bible Study Method—The Journey: Every follower of Christ needs to learn how to become a self-feeder of feasting on the pure Word of God for themselves. Every follower of Christ needs to become intimately acquainted with Jesus Himself. The Journey teaches the participant the inductive Bible study method of observation, interpretation, and application. This is done in an eight-week journey through the book of Luke, reading half a chapter per day, and learning how to journal and record what they are hearing as a fresh word from God every day.

5 Spiritual Preparation: The privilege of sharing the gospel of Christ with someone outside the faith is a supernatural undertaking. Jesus said that his disciples would receive the Holy Spirit, and then they would be His witnesses. This step in the process is designed to lead the participant to be filled with the compassion of Christ and the power of the Holy Spirit in order to prepare their heart for the work of sharing the good news of Jesus Christ.

6 Investing in Relationships: God has placed each of His followers into a network of relationships that are unique and providential. The very best prospects for personal evangelism and any local church are the people who are already in the network of relationships of the current members. This exercise will help the witness identify the people in the different areas of their life who need Christ so that they can intentionally invest in cultivating those relationships.

7 Praying for My Friends: The Holy Spirit is the one who convicts people of sin, draws them to Himself, takes the blinders off their spiritual eyes, reveals the gospel to them, gives them the gift of faith, and regenerates them. Because of this, prayer for our friends is essential in seeing them come to Christ. This step will equip the participant to pray according to the Word of God for their friends. In turn, they can then see the Holy Spirit perform the miracle of imparting the breath of new life into the hearts of those He will save.

8 Initiating Spiritual Conversation: We live in an age of relativism and existentialism in which a person's personal experience is their highest authority. Their experience must be respected as the witness draws out what is in their heart through Spirit-led listening. Since getting started in a spiritual conversation is the hardest part of sharing the gospel, the skill of having a list of good questions will give the witness confidence as they move from secular to spiritual conversations.

9 Sharing My Story: Because personal experience is so highly regarded in our culture of existentialism, a person's personal testimony of how they came to faith in Christ is a powerful tool in sharing the gospel. Sharing a person's personal faith journey will help someone identify and connect with a real-life story of faith. Using the Apostle Paul's testimony as a model, the witness will learn how to share what their life was like before Christ, how they came to Christ, and how their life has changed since receiving Christ.

CHAPTER 3

STEP 1 SHARING HIS STORY—STEPS TO KNOWING GOD

The uniqueness of Christianity, when compared with other world views, is found in the power of the death, burial, and resurrection of Jesus Christ, the Gospel. All other religions try to show us how to climb up the mountain to God. But in Christianity, God comes to us and does for us what we cannot do for ourselves. All other religions say "Do", but Christianity says "Done."

Discussing how to find peace with God and experience his purpose could be the most important discussion you will ever have.

STEPS TO KNOWING GOD

1. **Do you have an interest in spiritual things?**

2. **How would you describe your faith experience?**

3. **Do you have any particular spiritual beliefs?**

4. **Would you be willing to consider these Steps to Knowing God, his purpose for life and his promise for eternal life?**

UNDERSTANDING ESSENTIAL SPIRITUAL TRUTHS

CREATION: God loves you deeply, and He created you for a special purpose.

> **_God's love:_** *"For God so loved the world, that he gave his only Son, that whoever believes in him should not perish but have eternal life." (John 3:16)*

5. **How does it make you feel to know that God loved you so much that he gave His son Jesus to die for you?**

God's purpose:

> _[29] Jesus answered, "The most important is, 'Hear, O Israel: The Lord our God, the Lord is one. [30] And you shall love the Lord your God with all your heart and with all your soul and with all your mind and with all your strength.' [31] The second is this: 'You shall love your neighbor as yourself.' There is no other commandment greater than these." (Mark 12:29-31)_

6. What do you think about loving God and loving people as the highest purpose for your life?

BROKENNESS: We live in a broken world with broken dreams, broken relationships, and broken hearts.

7. How do you see brokenness in the world around you?

8. How have you seen brokenness in your life?

When sin came into the world, it created a broken world and separation from God. Every person has been separated from God because of an independent heart, which is expressed through passive indifference towards God or active rebellion against him.

> *Therefore, just as sin came into the world through one man, and death through sin, and so death spread to all men because all sinned - (Romans 5:12)*

> *...but your iniquities have made a separation between you and your God, and your sins have hidden his face from you so that he does not hear. (Isaiah 59:2)*

9.   The death referred to means eternal separation from God and eventual physical death. Why do you think it is hard for many people to admit that they have sinned against God and need forgiveness?

10.   If you could erase anything you regret about your past, what would you erase?

11.   Do you see a need for God's forgiveness?

RESTORATION: Jesus Christ died on the cross to pay the penalty for our sin so that we might be forgiven and restored in our relationship with God. Through His death, burial, and resurrection, He has bridged the gap of separation and made it possible to know God and walk in a new life with Him forever.

> *For Christ also suffered once for sins, the righteous for the unrighteous, that he might bring us to God, being put to death in the flesh but made alive in the spirit... (1 Peter 3:18)*

12. What does it mean to you personally to understand that Jesus Christ died on the cross to pay the penalty for your sin, so that you can be forgiven and enter into a relationship with God?

RESURRECTION: Through the resurrection of Christ, you can also be raised to walk in a new life with God.

> *Therefore, if anyone is in Christ, he is a new creation. The old has passed away; behold, the new has come. (2 Corinthians 5:17).*

13. If you know that you are placed in Christ, and He is living inside of you, how will that impact your ability to live the way you know God wants you to live?

RECEIVING CHRIST

To receive Christ, you need to admit, believe, change, and receive.

Admit: Agree with God that you have sinned and are in need of forgiveness.

14. How have you been independent from God, and what do you believe you need to be forgiven for?

Believe: Transfer your trust from what you have done, both good and bad to what Jesus Christ did for you on the cross.

15. Do you believe and embrace the truth that Jesus Christ died for your sin so you could be forgiven and reconciled to God?

Change: Trust the power of Christ in you to empower you to make the changes you know He wants you to make.

16. What kind of changes do you believe God wants you to make as you begin to follow Him?

17. Since you know you can't make those changes in your own strength, can you trust Christ to empower you to make those changes?

Receive: But to all who did receive him, who believed in his name, he gave the right to become children of God... (John 1:12)

Invite Christ to come into your life as your forgiver and the one who will control the direction of your life from this point forward.

18. Are you ready to receive Christ into your life?

Pray this prayer right now to receive Christ...

Dear Lord Jesus,

I need you. Thank you for loving me enough to die for me on the cross. I agree with you that I have sinned, and I need forgiveness. I confess the following ways I have been independent from you. (Go ahead and confess to God.) I transfer my trust from what I have done to what you did for me when you died on the cross for my sin. I believe your sacrifice for me is sufficient to forgive my sin and open up a relationship with you. I repent of my sin and trust you to empower me to make the following changes. (Tell God what changes you need to make.) I open my heart and invite you to come in and live your life inside of me through your Spirit. Thank you for saving me, and now I ask you to empower me to follow you in the fellowship and service of the church of Jesus Christ.

Amen

Look at what the Bible says about the commitment you just made.

"Just so, I tell you, there is joy before the angels of God over one sinner who repents." (Luke 15:10)

Heaven is throwing a party right now! Congratulations and welcome to God's family.

CHAPTER 4

STEP 2 DEEPER STUDY-LIFE'S MOST IMPORTANT QUESTION

INTRODUCTION

Most people believe that truth is found in each person's individual experience, or existentialism. Therefore, it is critical that we share the absolute truth of the Gospel in the context of a respectful dialogue. This conversational approach allows each person to read up to a question and then engage in a respectful dialogue about the answer. The paragraphs in the book following each question provide the Biblical answer to the question. The result of this conversation ends in a thorough explanation of The Gospel and a prayer of commitment to follow Jesus.

The benefits of beginning a discipleship relationship with a more in-depth look at the Gospel, with Life's Most Important Questions, are that you will be 'getting on the same page' using the basic message of the Christian faith, modeling how disciple-making begins with sharing the Gospel and training your friends how to share the Gospel with those they may disciple.

Now, you are ready to help lay the spiritual foundation to maturity, through follow-up, in the next step.

LIFE'S MOST IMPORTANT QUESTIONS

We can get so caught up in meeting the urgent demands of life that we fail to consider the most important questions concerning what life is all about. Are you just making a living or are you making a life? Are you just living to meet the demands of life or are you really living a meaningful, fulfilling life that is full of purpose and destiny?

This study gives you the opportunity to consider life's most important questions. Where did I come from? Who am I? Why am I here? Where am I going? The answers to these questions will unlock the keys to a meaningful, fulfilling life. We will use the Bible as the main resource in considering these questions.

1. What do you think about using the Bible as a reference for a consideration of life's most important questions?

Consider some reasons for using the Bible.

1. It is the best-selling book of all time and very respected as a guide for the deepest issues of life. It would be good to at least understand what it says about life's most important questions.
2. There are hundreds of prophecies or predictions in the Old Testament about things that would happen hundreds of years later, which were fulfilled in the New Testament in specific detail.
3. The writers of the Bible provide first-hand testimonies of the events they witnessed.

Let's consider what the Bible says about four of life's most important questions.

1 WHERE DID I COME FROM?

2. What is your opinion about where human life came from?

More important than the question of how or when human life originated is the question of who created us. The Bible teaches that every person was created by God as part of His good creation.

> *So God created man in his own image, in the image of God he created him; male and female he created them. (Genesis 1:27)*

> *...then the LORD God formed the man of dust from the ground and breathed into his nostrils the breath of life, and the man became a living creature. (Genesis 2:7)*

> *[21] So the LORD God caused a deep sleep to fall upon the man, and while he slept took one of his ribs and closed up its place with flesh. [22] And the rib that the LORD God had taken from the man he made into a woman and brought her to the man. (Genesis 2:21-22)*

3. What does it mean to you to know that you didn't just appear as a part of a random, meaningless process, but that you were purposefully designed by God himself?

2 WHO AM I?

4. In describing yourself, what characteristics would you use to answer the question, "Who am I?"

The Bible defines who we are in three ways.

> *A. Created in God's likeness:* We have been created in the likeness of God with a spiritual capacity, and we are very valuable to him. Therefore, every person should be treated with dignity and respect.
>
> *So God created man in his own image; in the image of God he created him; male and female he created them. (Genesis 1:27)*

5. What do you think it means to be created in the image of God?

Being created in His image means we have a spiritual capacity that other animals do not have. We have the capacity to relate to God.

6. Have you ever had any "God moments" or experiences in which you sensed God was speaking to you? What were they like?

7. What was your religious background like?

[13] For you created my inmost being; you knit me together in my mother's womb. [14] I praise you because I am fearfully and wonderfully made; your works are wonderful; I know that full well. [15] My frame was not hidden from you when I was made in the secret place, when I was woven together in the depths of the earth. [16] Your eyes saw my unformed body; all the days ordained for me were written in your book before one of them came to be. (Psalm 139:13-16 NIV)

8. What do these verses say about your self-worth?

B. Born into sin: Even though we were created in the image of God, because of the original sin of Adam, we were born into sin and our sin has separated us from God.

Therefore, just as sin came into the world through one man, and death through sin, and so death spread to all men because all sinned — (Romans 5:12)

The death referred to here means eventual physical death and the possibility of eternal separation from God.

9. Why do you think it is hard for many people to admit that they have sinned against God and need forgiveness?

...for all have sinned and fall short of the glory of God... (Romans 3:23)

Sin can be defined as independence from God by missing the mark of how He created us to live. It can be expressed as active rebellion through our actions, words or thoughts. It can also be expressed through a passive indifference of not pursuing a relationship with God.

10. If all have sinned, how many people does this include?

...but your iniquities have made a separation between you and your God, (Isaiah 59:2)

11. What do you think it means to be separated from God?

The Ten Commandments were given to us to show us our need for God, not to condemn us, or to provide an impossible standard we must keep in our own strength. Let's see how we measure up to the Ten Commandments.

1 "You shall have no other gods before me." (Exodus 20:3)

12. What are some things that have been more important to you than God?

2 "You shall not make for yourself a carved image, or any likeness of anything that is in heaven above, or that is in the earth beneath, or that is in the water under the earth." (Exodus 20:4)

13. What have you made for yourself that could be considered an idol?

3 *"You shall not take the name of the Lord your God in vain..." (Exodus 20:7)*

14. Have you ever taken the Lord's name in vain through profanity or irreverence?

4 *"Remember the Sabbath day, to keep it holy." (Exodus 20:8)*

15. Do you regularly set aside one day a week for worship and rest?

5 *"Honor your father and your mother..." (Exodus 20:12)*

16. Has there ever been a time when you did not honor or show respect to your parents?

6 "You shall not murder." (Exodus 20:13)

But Jesus said in Matthew 5:22, *"But I say to you that everyone who is angry with his brother will be liable to judgment"*

17. Have you ever been angry or felt hate towards anyone?

7 "You shall not commit adultery." (Exodus 20:14)

Jesus also said, "But I say to you that everyone who looks at a woman with lustful intent has already committed adultery with her in his heart." (Matthew 5:28)

18. Have you ever been guilty of lust?

8 "You shall not steal." (Exodus 20:15)

19. Have you ever taken something that did not belong to you, including stealing someone's reputation by what you said about them?

9 "You shall not bear false witness against your neighbor." (Exodus 20:16)

20. Have you ever lied about someone or to someone?

10 "You shall not covet..." (Exodus 20:17)

21. Have you ever coveted something someone else possessed?

The purpose of the Ten Commandments is not to condemn us or to raise an impossible standard, but to show us our need for forgiveness and grace.

22. After considering this, do you see a need for forgiveness and grace?

C. Given a new identity: Through forgiveness and grace, we can receive a new identity as children of God—the King of the Universe.

> *[4] But when the time had fully come, God sent his Son, born of a woman, born under law, [5] to redeem those under law, that we might receive the full rights of sons. [6] Because you are sons, God sent the Spirit of his Son into our hearts, the Spirit who calls out, "Abba, Father."[7] So you are no longer a slave, but a son; and since you are a son, God has made you also an heir. (Galatians 4:4-7, NIV)*

23. When you think of the privileges of the son of a king or queen of a relatively small nation like England, what would it do to your identity to know that you are the son or daughter of the King of the Universe?

3 WHY AM I HERE?

24. What would you say is your purpose in life, according to the way you are living it?

The Bible teaches us that God created us for a purpose, and that purpose is to love Him and to love our neighbor as ourselves both now and for all of eternity.

> *[28] And one of the scribes came up and heard them disputing with one another, and seeing that he answered them well, asked him. "Which commandment is the most important of all?"[29]Jesus answered, "The most important is, 'Hear, O Israel: The Lord our God, the Lord is one. [30]And*

you shall love the Lord your God with all your heart and with all your soul and with all your mind and with all your strength.'" (Mark 12:28-30)

25. How could you love God with your heart or emotions? Your soul or spirit? Your mind? Your strength?

26. Who is your neighbor? How can you love your neighbor?

27. How can your education or career be an expression of love for your neighbor? Share an example.

28. How can you love yourself without being selfish?

4 WHERE AM I GOING?

Life is moving towards a destiny. One day we will all die. *"And just as it is appointed for man to die once, and after that comes judgment..." (Hebrews 9:27)*

We will all face an eternal destiny.

29. How would you describe how long eternity is?

Someone compared eternity to a little bird picking up a grain of sand and flying off to another planet. If the bird waited one thousand years to come back and pick up the next grain, by the time the bird transferred all the grains of sand on earth to another planet, eternity would have just begun.

30. What do you think happens to a person's soul after they die?

The Bible teaches that every person will face an eternal destiny of either eternal punishment or eternal life.

[45] Then he will answer them, saying, 'Truly, I say to you, as you did not do it to one of the least of these, you did not do it to me.' [46] And these will go away into eternal punishment, but the righteous into eternal life." (Matthew 25:45-46)

31. If you were to die tonight, do you believe you would spend an eternity in heaven with God? Why do you believe this?

32. If God asked you to give Him a reason for allowing you to enter heaven, what would you say?

³ ...and said, "Truly, I say to you, unless you turn and become like children, you will never enter the kingdom of heaven. ⁴ Whoever humbles himself like this child is the greatest in the kingdom of heaven." (Matthew 18:3-4)

33. The childlike quality God is looking for is a simple, trusting, humble heart. Do you think you have a heart like that?

34. How would you describe your heart right now? Hard? Cold? Warm? Open? Trusting? Why?

The hope we have for eternal life is in what Jesus did for us. "For God so loved the world, that he gave his only Son, that whoever believes in him should not perish but have eternal life." (John 3:16)

THE TRUTH OF THE GOSPEL

If we want to know where we came from, who we are, why we are here, and where we are going, we need to understand some major truths in the Bible.

1 GOD: God is both loving and holy.

A) God is loving: God loves us, and He desires to have a relationship with us both now and in heaven for all of eternity. God, in the essence of His being, is love.

Anyone who does not love does not know God, because God is love. (1 John 4:8)

In this is love, not that we have loved God but that he loved us and sent his Son to be the propitiation for our sins. (1 John 4:10)

35. Could you ever love someone enough to allow your own child to die for them?

36. How does it make you feel to know that God loved you enough to send His son to die for you?

B) God is holy: God is also holy, and a sinful man cannot approach a holy God or enter heaven where there is no sin. Psalm 99:9 implores us to *"Exalt the Lord our God and worship at his holy mountain, for the Lord our God is holy!"*

The word "holy" in the original language means "to be cut apart or set apart." God is set apart from us in His sinlessness and purity.

37. When you see how righteous, holy, and pure God is, how does it make you feel about yourself in comparison?

There is no sin in heaven. As shared in *Revelation (21:27), "But nothing unclean will ever enter it, nor anyone who does what is detestable or false, but only those who are written in the Lamb's book of life."*

It's not a matter of the good in us outweighing the bad. One sin is enough to keep us out of heaven. As James states (2:10), "For whoever keeps the whole law but fails in one point has become guilty of all of it."

38. What dilemma does this create for us?

Since we all have sinned and there is no sin in heaven, we have a problem, but God did for us what we cannot do for ourselves by sending His son, Jesus. We need to understand who Jesus is and what He did for us.

2 CHRIST: Because our sin has separated us from God and we cannot save ourselves, God has solved this problem in the person and work of Jesus Christ.

39. What have you come to understand about who Jesus Christ is?

A) The person of Christ: Jesus Christ, as the only begotten Son of God, fully God and fully man, was born of a virgin, lived a sinless life, performed miracles, and fulfilled all of the Old Testament prophecies of the promised Messiah.

His deity – *"In the beginning was the Word, and the Word was with God, and the Word was God." (John 1:1)*

His humanity - *"And the Word became flesh and dwelt among us..." (John 1:14)*

His virgin birth – *[22]All this took place to fulfill what the Lord had spoken by the prophet: [23] "Behold, the virgin shall conceive and bear a son, and they shall call his name Immanuel" (which means, God with us). (Matthew 1:22-23)*

His sinless life - *As shared in 1 Peter 2:22, "He committed no sin, neither was deceit found in his mouth."*

His miracles - *"Men of Israel, hear these words: Jesus of Nazareth, a man attested to you by God with mighty works and wonders and signs that God did through him in your midst, as you yourselves know..." (Acts 2:22)*

His fulfillment of Messianic prophecies - *[36] For these things took place that the Scripture might be fulfilled: "Not one of his bones will be broken." (John 19:36)*

The events described in this passage in John 19 were the fulfillment of two Old Testament prophecies.

He keeps all his bones; not one of them is broken. (Psalm 34:20)

"And I will pour out on the house of David and the inhabitants of Jerusalem a spirit of grace and pleas for mercy, so that, when they look on me, on him whom they have pierced..." (Zechariah 12:10)

40. Do you believe these facts about the life of Christ?

B) The work of Christ. Jesus died on the cross to pay the penalty for our sins so that we might be forgiven. He was buried and rose again the third day to give us a new identity and the gift of eternal life. He has now ascended into heaven, where He intercedes for us and where He is preparing a place for us.

His death, burial, and resurrection -

> *³ For I delivered to you as of first importance what I also received: that Christ died for our sins in accordance with the Scriptures, ⁴ that he was buried, that he was raised on the third day in accordance with the Scriptures, ⁵ and that he appeared to Cephas, then to the twelve. ⁶ Then he appeared to more than five hundred brothers at one time..." (1 Corinthians 15:3-6)*

> *For Christ also suffered once for sins, the righteous for the unrighteous, that he might bring us to God... (1 Peter 3:18)*

41. What does it mean to you personally to understand that Jesus Christ died on the cross to pay the penalty for your sin, so that you can be forgiven and enter into a relationship with God?

We were buried therefore with him by baptism into death, in order that, just as Christ was raised from the dead by the glory of the Father, we too might walk in newness of life. (Romans 6:4)

Therefore, if anyone is in Christ, he is a new creation. The old has passed away; behold, the new has come. (2 Corinthians 5:17)

42. If your old sinful nature is crucified with Christ, and you have received the new life of Christ inside of you, how does that impact your ability to live the Christian life?

His ascension -

⁹ And when he had said these things, as they were looking on, he was lifted up, and a cloud took him out of their sight. ¹⁰ And while they were gazing into heaven as he went, behold, two men stood by them in white robes, ¹¹ and said, "Men of Galilee, why do you stand looking into heaven? This Jesus, who was taken up from you into heaven, will come in the same way as you saw him go into heaven." (Acts 1:9-11)

OUR RESPONSE

1 - GRACE:

We can only receive Jesus Christ by grace, through faith. Grace is the free gift of eternal life; therefore, it cannot be earned by any good works we may do.

NATURAL DISCIPLESHIP – 37

⁵ So too at the present time there is a remnant, chosen by grace. ⁶ But if it is by grace, it is no longer on the basis of works; otherwise grace would no longer be grace. (Romans 11:5-6)

⁸ For by grace you have been saved through faith. And this is not your own doing; it is the gift of God, ⁹ not a result of works, so that no one may boast. (Ephesians 2:8-9)

43. What are some of the good works people use to justify themselves before God?

44. Do you think there are any good works you have done that you could add to what Christ did for you on the cross? Please explain.

2 - FAITH:

We must individually receive Jesus Christ through faith by transferring our trust from what we have done to what Christ has done for us on the cross.

...know that a person is not justified by works of the law, but by faith in Jesus Christ. So we, too, have put our faith in Christ Jesus that we may be justified by faith in Christ and not by the works of the law, because by the works of the law no one will be justified. (Galatians 2:16 NIV)

45. Do you desire to transfer your trust from what you have done to what Christ has done for you?

3 - EVIDENCE:

The evidence that we have believed in Him will result in the following commitments:

We must receive Him personally into our lives as our forgiver and leader.

> *But to all who did receive him, who believed in his name, he gave the right to become children of God... (John 1:12)*

46. Do you desire to receive Christ into your life?

We must make a commitment to repent of our sins by trusting Christ in us to give us the power to make whatever changes He leads us to make.

> *For godly grief produces a repentance that leads to salvation without regret, whereas worldly grief produces death. (2 Corinthians 7:10)*

47. Do you desire to repent by trusting Christ to empower you to make whatever changes he wants you to make?

48. What kind of changes do you think God wants you to make?

We must follow Christ as His disciple, seeking to be obedient to His commands in the fellowship and service of His church, the Body of Christ.

And calling the crowd to him with his disciples, he said to them, "If anyone would come after me, let him deny himself and take up his cross and follow me." (Mark 8:34)

49. Do you desire to follow Christ in this way?

And he is the head of the body, the church. (Colossians 1:18)

...so we, though many, are one body in Christ, and individually members one of another. (Romans 12:5)

50. Do you desire to be a part of the Body of Christ, the church?

51. Has this Bible discussion made sense?

52. Do you have any questions about any of the points covered in this study?

53. Are you ready to receive Christ and to follow Him as his disciple? Can you explain why or why not?

The following prayer expresses a desire to ask Jesus Christ to be your Lord and Savior.

Dear Lord Jesus,

I need you. I have not lived my life according to your purposes. I confess that I have fallen short of your glory. I know that I need to be forgiven for my sin. Thank you for dying on the cross for my sin. I thank you that you promised to remove my sin as far as the east is from the west. I transfer my trust from what I have done to what Jesus did for me on the cross. I ask you to come into my life. I repent of my sin by trusting you to empower me to make the changes you want me to make. I want to follow you as your disciple. Thank you for coming into my life. Now make me the person you want me to be.

Amen

Does this prayer express the desire of your heart?

If it does, you can pray this prayer and God will hear and answer you according to His promise. Just pray this prayer right now, and God will honor your commitment.

Look at what the Bible says about the commitment you just made.

"Just so, I tell you, there is joy before the angels of God over one sinner who repents." (Luke 15:10)

Heaven is throwing a party right now. Congratulations and welcome to God's family!

CHAPTER 5

STEP 3 NEW BELIEVERS; GROUNDWORK SERIES

INTRODUCTION

If you observe the construction site of a high-rise building, what you see during the first months is people coming to work and disappearing down into a hole in the earth. When their foundation work is finished, a beautiful structure begins to appear. Often, our disciple-making efforts may seem to begin slowly with little evidence of progress.

But, if we are faithful, we will experience the beautiful work of the Holy Spirit as he produces Spiritual fruit in the lives of those we disciple. This step of developing a spiritual foundation is called follow-up or the basics.

This groundwork series includes six lessons that will build a strong foundation for you.

- Lesson 1 Receiving the Word
- Lesson 2 Assurance of Salvation
- Lesson 3 Victory Over Sin
- Lesson 4 Power for Living
- Lesson 5 The Cost of Discipleship
- Lesson 6 Disciplines of Grace

Welcome to the great adventure of doing the one thing Jesus Christ told us to do right before He ascended into heaven--to make disciples. We can find it very easy to fill our time doing many good things, but multiplying disciples of Christ is the best thing. This Groundwork Series was developed out of a desire to provide a resource that would provide conversation guides to facilitate a natural discussion of the most foundational truths for a growing follower of Christ.

This is not a book to read; it is a conversation to have. This material is designed to be read personally before each session, and then to read together during each session. It is very simple to use. Just take turns reading out loud until you come to a question. After reading each question, take the time to share your personal answers, respecting each person's perspective. This can be used in a small group setting, but it is most effective in a one-on-one or one-on-two setting. Personal discipleship provides the best accountability and relational dynamics. Jesus spent time with all twelve of his disciples, but He focused more on the inner circle of Peter, James and John. Jesus also clearly gave a higher priority to his relationship with John, who was called "the disciple who Jesus loved."

When you finish each session, it would be good to ask the question, "How can I pray for you?" This will keep your relationship personal. In turn, it will open many more opportunities for discipleship as you discuss and pray about the issues most pressing in your personal lives. Praying together is the essence of fellowship because you invite God into your conversation. These studies are a way to share your story, their story and God's story.

LESSON 1 - RECEIVING THE WORD

What kind of heart do you have when it comes to receiving the word of God? At the beginning of this study, it is good to consider the different ways people receive the word of God, because the way we receive the word of God will determine whether we grow as his followers or whether we get distracted and follow a different path.

> [4] *And when a great crowd was gathering and people from town after town came to him, he said in a parable,* [5]*"A Sower went out to sow his seed. And as he sowed, some fell along the path and*

was trampled underfoot, and the birds of the air devoured it. [6]And some fell on the rock, and as it grew up, it withered away, because it had no moisture. [7]And some fell among thorns, and the thorns grew up with it and choked it. [8]And some fell into good soil and grew and yielded a hundredfold." As he said these things, he called out, "He who has ears to hear, let him hear." [9]And when his disciples asked him what this parable meant, [10]he said, "To you it has been given to know the secrets of the kingdom of God, but for others they are in parables, so that 'seeing they may not see, and hearing they may not understand.' (Luke 8:4-10)

Jesus already knew what was in the hearts of those who gathered to hear him preach. These people had already rejected him, and he decided to respect their wishes and keep them in the darkness they loved so much. But he gave a reward to His true disciples. In Luke 8: 10 He said, "To you it has been given to know the secrets of the kingdom of God."

Jesus then teaches them a lesson about testing the soil of the heart. Look at the four types of soil which expose four kinds of different hearts revealing the way we receive God's word.

APPLYING THE WORD

1) The hard soil of a stolen heart:

[11] Now the parable is this: The seed is the word of God. [12]The ones along the path are those who have heard; then the devil comes and takes away the word from their hearts, so that they may not believe and be saved. (Luke 8:11-12)

Here, Jesus talks about how a farmer scatters seed in the field, but inevitably when he gets close to the edge of the field, some of the seed will fall on the hard path that has not been plowed up yet. This represents the hard soil of a stolen heart.

1. **How can you keep the truth of God's word from being stolen from your heart?**

I have stored up your word in my heart, that I might not sin against you.

(Psalm 119:11)

2. **How can you treat God's word as if it really is a treasure?**

2) The rocky soil of a tested heart.

> *And the ones on the rock are those who, when they hear the word, receive it with joy. But these have no root; they believe for a while, and in time of testing fall away. (Luke 8:13)*

Here, Jesus is referring to a shallow layer of soil on top of a hard layer of bedrock. The temptation of sin can be so strong that a person will give in and completely walk away from the truth they have received. A shallow commitment will lead a person to give in to temptation.

3. What kind of sin is the greatest temptation to you?

4. How can temptation cause us to walk away from the truth of God's word?

Whatever temporary pleasure sin brings you, it's not worth what you will lose. It's not worth losing your fellowship with God. It's not worth the natural consequences you will have to deal with as a result. It's not worth broken relationships with people who love you and care about you.

Another kind of temptation comes to those who receive the word with joy, and then they experience a time of affliction, adversity and trouble. The pain of suffering can be so disheartening and so discouraging; it can steal our hope and trust in the promises of God.

5. What kind of sufferings and struggles are you presently going through?

6. **How do they make you feel about your relationship with God?**

For because he himself has suffered when tempted, he is able to help those who are being tempted. (Hebrews 2:18)

7. **According to this verse, how does Jesus relate to us in our suffering?**

God will use suffering to refine our character, to purify our hearts, to temper us, to strengthen us and make us stronger. An athlete does not get faster and stronger without the pain and suffering of breaking down muscles so they can be built back stronger. Your suffering is not an indication that God has forsaken you. It is actually an indication that He loves you.

And after you have suffered a little while, the God of all grace, who has called you to his eternal glory in Christ, will himself restore, confirm, strengthen, and establish you. (1 Peter 5:10)

8. **How do you believe God wants to use suffering in your life?**

3) *The thorny soil of a distracted heart.*

> *And as for what fell among the thorns, they are those who hear, but as they go on their way they are choked by the cares and riches and pleasures of life, and their fruit does not mature. (Luke 8:14)*

The thorns and weeds not only choked out the stalk of the good plants, but they also choked out the roots. Life's worries, riches, and pleasures will choke out the priority of regularly receiving the word of God and the time and energy needed to carry it out. Some examples of this could be demanding work schedules, all the activities that our kids are involved in, get-rich-quick schemes, sensual pursuits, the lust for more possessions, hobbies, the lake, the beach, relatives, friends, and the prideful drive for recognition and achievement.

9. What is it that distracts you from pursuing God in your personal time alone with him in his word?

10. What is it that distracts you from coming to church to pursue the teaching of God's word?

11. How can you keep your heart from being distracted by worry, riches, and pleasure?

4) The fertile soil of a noble heart.

As for that in the good soil, they are those who, hearing the word, hold it fast in an honest and good heart, and bear fruit with patience. (Luke 8:15)

The person with a noble and good heart is a person who does three things with the word of God. He hears it, retains it, and perseveres in obeying it.

12. Which of the four kinds of hearts best represents your life right now?

13. What actions are needed to cultivate a good and noble heart?

LESSON 2 - ASSURANCE OF SALVATION

Do you think it is possible to know for certain that you will spend eternity in heaven? Assurance of salvation is very important because there are many doubts that can fill the mind of a professing Christian. You can wonder if you really belong in the Christian faith. You can doubt that God really has given you eternal life.

14. How sure are you right now that if you died today, you would go to heaven? Why?

0%___ 25%___ 50%___ 75%___ 100%___

We can have confidence that Christ truly has given us the gift of eternal life. Gaining assurance of salvation comes to us in two ways.

1 - Confidence in the Promises of God in his Word

You have been saved by grace through faith.

> *[8]For by grace you have been saved through faith. And this is not your own doing; it is the gift of God, [9]not a result of works, so that no one may boast. (Ephesians 2:8-9)*

Grace is God's unmerited favor. There is nothing we can do to earn or deserve it. To be saved is to be delivered from the penalty of sin. There is nothing we can do to erase our sin. Jesus paid it all! We are saved by grace, through faith as we transfer our trust from what we have done, to what Christ did for us on the cross.

15.   What are some good works people often try to do to get into heaven?

You have become a new creature in Christ:

Therefore, if anyone is in Christ, he is a new creation. The old has passed away; behold, the new has come. (2 Corinthians 5:17)

16. If you are a new person in Christ, what are some of the old things in your life that have passed away, and what are some of the new things that have come?

All of your sins have been forgiven:

For Christ also suffered once for sins, the righteous for the unrighteous, that he might bring us to God, being put to death in the flesh but made alive in the spirit... (1 Peter 3:18)

17.   What does it mean to you to know that all of your sins have been forgiven and Jesus Christ has brought you across the great divide of separation between God and man?

Christ will never leave you or forsake you:

> *Keep your life free from love of money, and be content with what you have, for he has said, "I will never leave you nor forsake you." (Hebrews 13:5)*

18. Can you remember a time when you felt deserted or forsaken by someone you trusted? Describe it.

19. How does it make you feel to know that Jesus will never desert you or forsake you?

Christ has given you eternal life:

> *^{27} My sheep hear my voice, and I know them, and they follow me. ^{28} I give them eternal life, and they will never perish, and no one will snatch them out of my hand. ^{29} My Father, who has given them to me, is greater than all, and no one is able to snatch them out of the Father's hand. (John 10:27-29)*

20.   According to this promise, why can you have confidence that you will never lose the gift of eternal life?

2 – Evidence of True Belief

¹² Whoever has the Son has life; whoever does not have the Son of God does not have life. ¹³ I write these things to you who believe in the name of the Son of God, that you may know that you have eternal life. (1 John 5:12-13)

21.   Did God promise that we can only hope that we might have eternal life, or that we can know?

If John wrote "these things" in order that you might know you have eternal life, it is necessary to know what "these things" are. "These things" he is referring to is everything he wrote in the book of 1 John up to that point. The whole book of 1 John is a series of evidence for a genuine Christian. If you read the whole book, you will find there are three primary characteristics that will be present in the life of a true believer. He is not saying that doing "these things" will save us. He is saying that "these things" are going to be evident in the life of a true believer. So what are "these things?" There are three evidences for a genuine Christian.

The evidence of believing the truth:

> [5] *This is the message we have heard from him and proclaim to you, that God is light, and in him is no darkness at all.* [6] *If we say we have fellowship with him while we walk in darkness, we lie and do not practice the truth.* [7] *But if we walk in the light, as he is in the light, we have fellowship with one another, and the blood of Jesus his Son cleanses us from all sin. (1 John 1:5-7)*

22.   According to verse seven, if you are walking in the light of truth, then what will you believe in that will cleanse you from all sin?

The evidence of obedience:

> [3] *And by this we know that we have come to know him, if we keep his commandments.* [4] *Whoever says "I know him" but does not keep his commandments is a liar, and the truth is not in him... (1 John 2:3-4)*

23.   What does this say about the person who defiantly refuses to obey the commands of Christ?

24. What would you need to do in order to demonstrate that you are seeking to obey the commands of Christ?

The evidence of love for the church:

We know that we have passed out of death into life, because we love the brothers. Whoever does not love abides in death. (1 John 3:14)

The term "brothers" here refers to the church.

25. If this is so, then what would we need to do to demonstrate that we love our brothers and sisters in the church?

[24] And let us consider how to stir up one another to love and good works, [25] not neglecting to meet together, as is the habit of some, but encouraging one another, and all the more as you see the Day drawing near. (Hebrews 10:24)

26. According to this verse, why is it important that we are involved regularly in gathering together with the church for worship and fellowship?

Our confidence is ultimately in the trustworthiness of God and His promises.

14 And this is the confidence that we have toward him, that if we ask anything according to his will he hears us. 15 And if we know that he hears us in whatever we ask, we know that we have the requests that we have asked of him. (1 John 5:14-15)

If you have believed in the truth that the blood of Jesus can cleanse you from your sin, if you are seeking to demonstrate love and involvement with your brothers and sisters in the church, and if it is your desire to demonstrate obedience to the commands of Christ, then according to his promise you can know for sure that you have the gift of eternal life.

27. After this study, how sure are you right now that if you died today, you would go to heaven?

0%__ 25%__ 50%__ 75%__ 100%__

LESSON 3 - VICTORY OVER SIN

Do you believe it is possible to overcome the power of sin? During this study, we will see that even though we were born into sin and separated from our Creator, Christ defeated the power of sin through his sinless life, his sacrificial death, and his victorious resurrection. As believers in Christ, we have the ability to confess, repent, and be forgiven of our sins. This is a liberating truth we can rely on as we walk in victory.

Sin and Separation from God

Before you became a Christian, even though you were created in the image of God and were part of his good creation, you were also alienated from God because you were born into sin and because you practiced sin.

As King David said in *Psalm 51:5, "Behold, I was brought forth in iniquity, and in sin did my mother conceive me."*

Our sin caused us to be separated from God.

> *...but your iniquities have made a separation between you and your God, and your sins have hidden His face from you so that He does not hear. (Isaiah 59:2)*

28. Why do you think it is hard for people to admit that they are sinners and are in need of a Savior?

Reconciliation through Christ

When you received Jesus Christ and trusted in what He did for you on the cross, everything changed. The penalty of your sin was forgiven, and you became a child of God.

> *But to all who did receive Him, who believed in his name, He gave the right to become children of God... (John 1:12)*

At this point, you have entered into a new relationship with God as his child and as a member of his family, the church. When you received Christ, something happened to your old sinful nature.

> *We know that our old self was crucified with Him in order that the body of sin might be brought to nothing, so that we would no longer be enslaved to sin. (Romans 6:6)*

29. According to this passage, what happened to your old nature when you received Christ?

Your nature is the essence of who you are. You are now no longer identified as a sinner, but it is important to know that you will continue to struggle with the power of sin in your life. This is called the principle of indwelling sin or the flesh. While it does not define you in your identity, it is still a very strong force in your life. Paul expressed it this way.

> *[18] For I know that nothing good dwells in me, that is, in my flesh. For I have the desire to do what is right, but not the ability to carry it out. [19] For I do not do the good I want, but the evil I do not*

want is what I keep on doing. [20] *Now if I do what I do not want, it is no longer I who do it, but sin that dwells within me. (Romans 7:18-20)*

The word sin comes from a Greek word which means "to miss the mark". As shared in Romans 3:23, "for all have sinned and fall short of the glory of God..."

Since sin is falling short of his glory, it can be anything that would cause you to be independent from God. It can be active rebellion, passive indifference, things you say, things you do, even thoughts and motives that fall short of living to glorify God in every part of your life.

30. What are some of the good things you want to do that are hard to establish as regular habits?

31. What are some of the things you do not want to do that you are having a hard time stopping?

Relationship vs. Fellowship

You can now know that sin need not have dominion over you. Because you have died to a sinful way of living, you can recognize that before you became a Christian, you sinned because you had to. It was your nature. Now that your old self has been crucified with Christ, if you sin, it is because you choose to. But you have a new source of power that allows you to have victory over the dominion of sin in your life.

> *[11] So you also must consider yourselves dead to sin and alive to God in Christ Jesus. [12] Let not sin therefore reign in your mortal body, to make you obey its passions. [13] Do not present your members to sin as instruments for unrighteousness, but present yourselves to God as those who have been brought from death to life, and your members to God as instruments for righteousness. [14] For sin will have no dominion over you, since you are not under law but under grace. (Romans 6:11-14)*

32. What hope does this passage give you that you truly can have victory over the power of sin in your life?

Nothing can ever change the fact that you are God's adopted child, and your relationship with God can never be broken, but it is possible for your fellowship with God to be broken. When a child disobeys their parent, it will not change their name or the fact that he or she is still the child of that father or mother, but it is possible for the fellowship between parent and child to be broken, and the child will have to apologize before the fellowship can be restored.

If I had cherished iniquity in my heart, the Lord would not have listened. (Psalm 66:18)

The Bible teaches us that our fellowship can be restored when we immediately respond in genuine brokenness, confession, and repentance.

Brokenness, Confession....

The sacrifices of God are a broken spirit; a broken and contrite heart, O God, you will not despise. (Psalm 51:17)

23 Search me, O God, and know my heart! Try me and know my thoughts! 24 And see if there be any grievous way in me, and lead me in the way everlasting! (Psalm 139:23-24)

33. Do you see remorse, humility, and brokenness as a positive experience or a negative experience?

34. How does it make you feel to know you don't have to be afraid of your heart, and you can even ask God to identify things He wants you to change?

Once we have become aware of something that has broken our fellowship with God, we can embrace the pain of conviction, and quickly confess it to the Lord.

> *If we confess our sins, he is faithful and just to forgive us our sins and to cleanse us from all unrighteousness. (1 John 1:9)*

To confess means "to say the same" or "to agree." When we confess, we simply agree with God that we have fallen short of his glory in a specific way. We naturally hate to admit that we are wrong. It's easy for our defense mechanism to kick in and we try to justify ourselves. But, if we can come to a place of being quick to recognize our sin and to even ask God to search us and show us if there is anything we need to deal with, we will be on a fast track pathway to growth. Confession truly is good for the soul!

As a response to this teaching, why don't you take a piece of paper, write out every sin you can recall that God has convicted you of, write 1 John 1:9 across the piece of paper, and then tear it up and throw it away.

> *...as far as the east is from the west, so far does he remove our transgressions from us. (Psalm 103:12)*

Notice it doesn't say "as far as the north is from the south," because there is a definite north pole and a definite south pole, but the direction of east and west is limitless. Even if you don't feel forgiven after you confess, you can thank God by faith that he has forgiven you and trust your emotions to catch up to the truth of his promise.

35. What kind of freedom does it give you to know that your sin has been completely erased, and God will remember it no more?

... And Repentance

The final step in gaining victory over sin is repentance. To repent means to change your mind and direction of living by turning from only pleasing self to loving God and others. We are called to not just confess our sin, but to repent of it.

> *Whoever conceals his transgressions will not prosper, but he who confesses and forsakes them will obtain mercy. (Proverbs 28:13)*

> *For godly grief produces a repentance that leads to salvation without regret, whereas worldly grief produces death. (2 Corinthians 7:10)*

36.   What do you think is the difference between a sorrow the world produces and the sorrow God produces?

Repentance is choosing to trust the indwelling presence of Christ in your life to empower you to make the changes he wants you to make. If you try to repent in your own strength, you will be sure to fail, and then you will have to repent of the way you are repenting. But, when you trust Christ to give you the power to change, you are operating according to his power and not your own. You can then step out in obedience. Even if it is hard to change, you can continue to trust God to give you the strength you need.

Repentance means changing your mind and going in a new direction. Before you came to Christ, the world was in front of you and God was behind you, but repentance is putting God in front of you and the world behind you.

37. What changes do you think God wants you to make as you trust Him to give you power?

Sometimes when a child disobeys his parent, part of the discipline will be a time-out to think about what he has done. There is a time in which the parent may still be angry and there is a distance between the discipline and the restoring of fellowship. God does not give time-outs. He wants you back in his lap the instant you are aware of anything that is not pleasing to him. You can be sure that God does not want any time to elapse between your sin and your restoration.

The ultimate victory over sin will happen when Jesus comes for us.

Beloved, we are God's children now, and what we will be has not yet appeared; but we know that when he appears we shall be like him, because we shall see him as he is. (1 John 3:2)

We have been saved from the penalty of sin. That is called *justification*. We are being saved from the power of sin. That is called *sanctification*. One day we will be saved from the presence of sin. That is called *glorification*.

38. How does it make you feel to know that the day is coming, when you see Jesus face to face, when you will never disappoint God again?

LESSON 4 - POWER FOR LIVING

Trying to live the Christian life in your own strength, apart from the power of the Holy Spirit, is like lighting a cabin with candles next to a hydro-electric plant. Some people are reluctant to receive Christ because they do not believe they will be able to keep the commitment. They are right. There is only one man who has fully kept the commitment and lived the perfect Christian life. It was Jesus Christ, and even He said, "I can do nothing apart from the Father."

That is why we must rely on the power of the Spirit of Christ to work in us and through us. In this lesson we will see how we receive the promised Holy Spirit, what it means to be filled with the Spirit and the blessings that come from yielding to the Holy Spirit.

The Promise of the Holy Spirit

When Jesus came to the end of His life on this earth, He made a powerful promise to the disciples.

> *[16] And I will ask the Father, and he will give you another Helper, to be with you forever, [17] even the Spirit of truth, whom the world cannot receive, because it neither sees him nor knows him. You know him, for he dwells with you and will be in you. (John 14:16-17)*

Jesus knew that he was going back to the Father and that He had an even better plan. His plan was that the Holy Spirit, the third person of the trinity, would be everything to the disciples that Jesus was to them in his physical presence. It was even better that the Holy Spirit was sent because Jesus was limited to a physical body and could only be in one place at a time, but the Holy Spirit is omnipresent, everywhere at the same time. The Holy Spirit would indwell every believer with His presence and power. Since he is the Spirit of Christ, he is the indwelling presence of Christ.

> *Nevertheless, I tell you the truth: it is to your advantage that I go away, for if I do not go away, the Helper will not come to you. But if I go, I will send him to you. (John 16:7)*

¹³ When the Spirit of truth comes, he will guide you into all the truth, for he will not speak on his own authority, but whatever he hears he will speak, and he will declare to you the things that are to come. (John 16:13)

39. What hope does it give you to know that you have not been left to live the Christian life in your own strength?

Receiving the Holy Spirit

At the moment of receiving Christ, the Bible says we were born again. We were born once physically, but now we have been born spiritually. Before we received Christ, our spirits were dead and lifeless like a deflated balloon. But then we were convicted by the Holy Spirit of our need for forgiveness. He then breathed the breath of life into our spirits, regenerating us, taking the blinders off of our eyes to see and understand the gospel, and giving us the gift of faith to believe in the gospel of Jesus Christ.

> *For in one Spirit we were all baptized into one body – Jews or Greeks, slaves or free – and all were made to drink of one Spirit. (1 Corinthians 12:13)*

> *You, however, are not in the flesh but in the Spirit, if in fact the Spirit of God dwells in you. Anyone who does not have the Spirit of Christ does not belong to him. (Romans 8:9)*

At the moment of salvation, we received the Holy Spirit and we were immersed by the Holy Spirit into the body of Christ, the church. He now lives in us and desires to be released in and through us as we walk in the Spirit by His presence and power.

40. How does it impact your ability to live the Christian life now that you know the Holy Spirit lives inside of you and is promising to release His power in and through you?

Being Filled with the Holy Spirit

The receiving of the Holy Spirit, or the baptism of the Holy Spirit, is a once in a lifetime event that does not have to be repeated. We are indwelt by his presence at the moment of salvation, and He will never leave us or forsake us. However, as we live out the Christian life, we do need to be continually filled with the Holy Spirit. The filling of the Holy Spirit is the experience of receiving the presence and power of the Holy Spirit as we give Him complete control of our lives. The filling of the Holy Spirit is not needed because He leaks out of us. We do not need to get more of Him, but we need to yield more of our lives to His control.

> *And do not get drunk with wine, for that is debauchery, but be filled with the Spirit, (Ephesians 5:18)*

The grammatical construction of this verse could be rendered, "Be ye being filled on a continuous basis." We are filled by the Holy Spirit by exercising what someone has called spiritual breathing. We exhale by confessing any known sin to the Lord. We inhale by yielding the different areas of our lives to his control and asking him to fill us with His presence and power in each of those areas.

41. How would you describe the difference between the baptism of the Holy Spirit and the filling of the Holy Spirit?

42. What areas of your life can you yield to the control of the Holy Spirit? (See list below.)

- You can yield your mind to His control, asking Him to expose the lies of the enemy and replace them with His truth. You can invite Him to be free to place His thoughts in your mind as you fill it up with the truth of His word.

- You can yield your tongue to His control so that your speech will build up and not tear down.

- You can yield your emotions to His control so that you weep over the things He weeps over and rejoice over the things He rejoices over.

- You can yield your will to His control so that you will make decisions that would glorify God, trusting that He is at work both to will and do what is pleasing to Him. That means He can and will empower you to make wise choices.

- You can yield your body to His control, both in the maintenance of your body as the temple of the Holy Spirit and in the ministry of your body, using your energy to serve God.

- You can yield your personality to His control letting, Him use you to be His special agent of love.

- You can yield your strengths and weaknesses to His control, trusting Him to use your strengths for good and letting His strength be perfected in your weaknesses.

- You can yield your finances to His control, seeing yourself as a steward of His resources.

43.   How will these areas of your life be different when you yield them to the control and the filling of the Holy Spirit?

Natural, Carnal and Spiritual

The natural person does not accept the things of the Spirit of God, for they are folly to him, and he is not able to understand them because they are spiritually discerned. (1 Corinthians 2:14)

But I, brothers, could not address you as spiritual people, but as people of the flesh, as infants in Christ. (1 Cor. 3:1)

These two verses talk about three kinds of people. It talks about the natural man, the carnal man and the spiritual man. The natural man is a man who is still separated from God and is without Christ. Christ is outside of his life and his own ego is still in control. The carnal man is a person who has received Christ but has not yielded complete control of his life to Christ as Lord. He is not growing and is still living according to his own strength. The spiritual man is a person who is in the process of yielding every area of his life to the control of the Spirit of Christ and is seeking to allow the Holy Spirit to direct and empower him to live a life of obedience to God.

44. Would you describe yourself as a Natural Man ____ Carnal Man____ or Spiritual Man____?

45. Which kind of person would you like to be?

46. Are you ready to yield complete control of your life to Christ and to ask God to fill you with His Holy Spirit?

Consider the following prayer:

Dear Lord,

I want to resign as the general manager of my life and turn that management over to you. I want to deny myself the right to control my life and release that control to you. I want to take up my cross, dying to self every day, and I want to follow you and your ways through submitting to the authority of your word. I ask you to fill me with the Holy Spirit right now as I yield all of the areas of my life to your control. I yield my mind, my tongue, my emotions, my will, my body, my personality, my strengths and weaknesses and even my finances to your control. I now trust you to fill me with the power of the Holy Spirit. As I walk in obedience to your commands, I thank you by faith that you have just filled me with your Spirit.

Amen

Does this prayer represent the desire of your heart? You can pray it right now and He has promised He will hear and answer. Pray it out loud, phrase by phrase and God will hear the desire of your heart.

[14] And this is the confidence that we have toward him, that if we ask anything according to his will he hears us. [15] And if we know that he hears us in whatever we ask, we know that we have the requests that we have asked of him. (1 John 5:14-15)

We know it is God's will to be filled with the Spirit because He commanded it.

47. Did you ask him to fill you with the Spirit?

If so, you can thank him by faith that you have been filled. You do not need to look for a tingling in your spine, but rather receive His filling by faith, thanking God that He filled you with His Spirit and start walking in the Spirit. This is an exercise you can do every day for the rest of your life. Just enter into spiritual breathing by exhaling as you confess your sin, surrender control to Him, ask Him to fill you with His presence and power, and receive it by faith.

LESSON 5 - THE COST OF DISCIPLESHIP

Jesus did not distinguish between being a Christian and being a disciple. He simply challenged those who would be His followers to count the cost. Many people want to be Christians on their own terms, but as we will see in this lesson, this is not an option. We must recognize that following Jesus is challenging, but it is worth it. In this study, we will seek to understand what it really means to follow Christ and we will examine our own lives according to His definition of a disciple.

Count the Cost

During the ministry of Jesus, His popularity grew, and great crowds were following Him, but He was not impressed by their enthusiasm. He knew that most of those in the crowd were not the least bit interested in spiritual things. Some wanted only to see miracles, others heard that He fed the hungry, and a few hoped He would overthrow Rome and establish David's promised kingdom. They were expecting the wrong things. Jesus turned to the multitude and preached a sermon that deliberately thinned out the ranks.

If you were in the crowd that day, would you be one of the ones who turned and walked away, or would you be one who stepped up to the challenge and continued following Jesus as His disciple? Jesus called people to count the cost of what it means to be a true follower of Him. In this study, we are challenged with what it means to be a true disciple of Christ. He calls us to make Him lord of every area of our lives.

Dietrich Bonhoeffer, a pastor in Germany during Hitler's reign, was imprisoned and died for his faith. In his book, The Cost of Discipleship, he said "Salvation is free, but discipleship will cost you your life."

> *[25] Now great crowds accompanied him, and he turned and said to them, [26] "If anyone comes to me and does not hate his own father and mother and wife and children and brothers and sisters, yes, and even his own life, he cannot be my disciple. [27] Whoever does not bear his own cross and come after me cannot be my disciple. [28] For which of you, desiring to build a tower, does not first sit down and count the cost, whether he has enough to complete it? [29] Otherwise, when he has laid a foundation and is not able to finish, all who see it begin to mock him, [30] saying, 'This man began to build and was not able to finish.' [31] Or what king, going out to encounter another king in war, will not sit down first and deliberate whether he is able with ten thousand to meet him who comes against him with twenty thousand? [32] And if not, while the other is yet a great way off, he sends a delegation and asks for terms of peace. [33] So therefore, any one of you who does not renounce all that he has cannot be my disciple. (Luke 14:25-33)*

The term "hate" here literally means "to love less." Jesus is saying our love for Him should be so strong that any other love we have for our closest family members, or even ourselves, would look like hatred in comparison.

48. How would you compare the love you have for your immediate family members to your love for Jesus?

49. If a cross represents an instrument of death, what do you think it means to take up your cross?

50. If you count the cost of what it means to be a true disciple of Christ, how will it help you to keep from falling away from Christ and His church?

51. What do you think it means to give up all your possessions in order to be a disciple of Christ?

Take Up Your Cross

[24] Then Jesus told his disciples, "If anyone would come after me, let him deny himself and take up his cross and follow me. [25] For whoever would save his life will lose it, but whoever loses his life for my sake will find it. [26] For what will it profit a man if he gains the whole world and forfeits his soul? Or what shall a man give in return for his soul? (Matthew 16:24-26)

To deny yourself means to resign as the general manager of your life and turn that management over to Christ. It means to give up the right to control your life and give control to Christ. Jesus isn't satisfied to be just one of the spokes in the wheel of our lives, but He calls us to make Him the hub to which everything is connected and around which everything revolves.

Jim Elliott was a missionary to the Auca Indians who was killed by them as he was seeking to establish a relationship. Before he died, he said, "A man is no fool who gives up what he cannot keep to gain what he cannot lose."

Consider some of the following areas of your life: Career, family, relationships, future plans, house, car, hobbies, free time, fitness and exercise, investment portfolio, retirement fund and material possessions that are important to you.

52. What are some of the areas of your life that would be hard for you to give up control to Christ?

53. How can you save your life by losing it?

54. What is an example of gaining the whole world in exchange for your soul?

Follow Jesus

⁹ As Jesus passed on from there, he saw a man called Matthew sitting at the tax booth, and he said to him, "Follow me." And he rose and followed him. ¹⁰ And as Jesus reclined at table in the house, behold, many tax collectors and sinners came and were reclining with Jesus and his disciples. (Matthew 9:9-10)

Jesus called Matthew to follow Him. Matthew got up and followed Him, and according to this passage, in the very next scene, Jesus is sitting at Matthew's house eating with Matthew's friends. If this is the case, what did it mean for Matthew to follow Jesus? It would seem that part of what it means to follow Jesus is to reach out within our existing relationships, sharing the love of Christ with those we know in a natural way. The gospel is spread most naturally through circles of existing relationships.

55. If you were going to invite your friends who do not know Jesus over for dinner, who would you invite?

³¹ So Jesus said to the Jews who had believed him, "If you abide in my word, you are truly my disciples, ³² and you will know the truth, and the truth will set you free." (John 8:31-32)

56. What do you think it means to continue in the word of Christ?

57. How can you be set free by knowing the truth of the word of Christ?

¹⁸ While walking by the Sea of Galilee, he saw two brothers, Simon (who is called Peter) and Andrew his brother, casting a net into the sea, for they were fishermen. ¹⁹ And he said to them, "Follow me, and I will make you fishers of men." ²⁰ Immediately they left their nets and followed him. (Matthew 4:18-20)

To follow Jesus is to become a fisher of men. To be a fisher of men is to seek to influence as many people as possible to enter into a relationship with Christ. Is it possible that too many Christians are no longer fishers of men but keepers of the aquarium?

58. What are some ways you can become a fisher of men?

¹⁵ When they had finished breakfast, Jesus said to Simon Peter, "Simon, son of John, do you love me more than these?" He said to him, "Yes, Lord; you know that I love you." He said to him, "Feed my lambs." ¹⁶ He said to him a second time, "Simon, son of John, do you love me?" He said to him, "Yes, Lord; you know that I love you." He said to him, "Tend my sheep." ¹⁷ He said to him the third time, "Simon, son of John, do you love me?" Peter was grieved because he said to him the third time, "Do you love me?" and he said to him, "Lord, you know everything; you know that I love you." Jesus said to him, "Feed my sheep." (John 21:15-17)

This is the first heart to heart conversation Jesus had with Peter after His resurrection, after Peter, one of His closest disciples, had denied Him. It has been suggested that Jesus asked Peter if he loved him three times, once for each time Peter had denied Him. In order for Peter to show his love for Jesus, he was instructed to care for the sheep of Jesus. The sheep of Jesus are His children, those who are also followers of Christ.

59. What are some ways you can tend, care for, and shepherd the sheep of Jesus?

60. If caring for your brothers and sisters in the church is a way you can show your love for Christ, how does that change the way you feel about serving in practical ways as you care for the family of God?

61. After seeing the cost of discipleship, are you ready to make the kind of commitment to Christ that will identify you as a genuine disciple of His?

62. Which of the marks of a disciple do you think will be the most challenging to fulfill?

It is wonderful to know that we have not been left to follow Christ as his disciples in our own strength. God is calling us to simply yield control of our lives to Him, and to trust the Spirit of Christ in us to empower us to follow Him in joyful obedience as we pour out our lives in loving God and loving others.

LESSON 6 THE DISCIPLINES OF GRACE

A disciple is one who disciplines himself to follow the commands of Christ. If we are going to grow into fully mature followers of Christ, we must adopt certain disciplines that will allow us to experience our highest potential in the kingdom of God. Just as an athlete or a musician must enter into certain disciplines in order to master the skills necessary to excel, a Christian must enter into certain disciplines that will be an expression of our love for Christ.

> *[26] So I do not run aimlessly; I do not box as one beating the air. [27] But I discipline my body and keep it under control, lest after preaching to others I myself should be disqualified. (1 Corinthians 9:26-27)*

> *...train yourself for godliness... (1 Timothy 4:7)*

63.   According to these verses, what can you hope to accomplish if you adopt the disciplines of the faith?

And God is able to make all grace abound to you, so that having all sufficiency in all things at all times, you may abound in every good work. (2 Corinthians 9:8)

64.   Why do we call them disciplines of grace?

When we walk and live in the grace of God, He gives us the inner sufficiency and abundance we need for all the good deeds we do. The grace of God is His unmerited favor. We do not exercise discipline to earn God's favor, but we do it out of the motivations of grace. The proper motivations of grace are gratefulness for the past grace of God, love for the present grace of God and hope for the future grace of God. Make sure you always exercise discipline for the right motives.

65.   If you exercise discipline out of a motivation of grace instead of trying to exercise discipline to earn God's favor, what kind of attitude will you have?

Personal Disciplines

Bible Study:

> *¹ Blessed are those whose way is blameless, who walk in the law of the LORD! ² Blessed are those who keep his testimonies, who seek him with their whole heart... (Psalm 119:1-2)*

> *I will delight in your statutes; I will not forget your word. (Psalm 119:16)*

The word of God is our very life. It was intended by God to be just as nourishing to our souls as food is to our bodies. A botanist will dissect a flower and examine it scientifically but a bee simply extracts the sweet nectar from it. Do you want to be a botanist or a bee? We need to come to God's word with a desperate desire to hear a fresh, personal word from Him.

66. How can the Bible become a delight for you instead of just a discipline?

> *All scripture is breathed out by God and profitable for teaching, for reproof, for correction, and for training in righteousness... (2 Timothy 3:16)*

> *For the word of God is living and active, sharper than any two-edged sword, piercing to the division of soul and of spirit, of joints and of marrow, and discerning the thoughts and intentions of the heart. (Hebrews 4: 12)*

God has given you His word for a purpose. His word will take you on a continual course of growth as you allow it to teach you, reprove you, correct you, and train you in righteousness. It is beneficial to get on a Bible reading plan that will allow you to read all the way through the Bible. As you come into the presence of God, the fastest way to hear His voice is to just jump right into his word. A simple approach is to read, underline the verses that really speak to you, and then pray them back to God. His word is powerful and will accomplish its purpose if we saturate our lives with it.

67. How important is it for you to spend time in God's word every day?

68. What kind of Bible study plan are you involved in right now?

69. Where would you like to be one year from now in your plan to study God's word?

Prayer: Prayer is the place you absorb and release the power of God. It is both speaking to God and listening for His voice through impressions in your mind.

...do not be anxious about anything, but in everything by prayer and supplication with thanksgiving let your requests be made known to God. (Philippians 4:6)

70. What is the best thing you can do about your fears and anxieties?

71. What do you think it will do to your fears if you immediately transform every anxious thought into a prayer?

Therefore, confess your sins to one another and pray for one another, that you may be healed. The prayer of a righteous person has great power as it is working. (James 5:16)

You do not pray to get God moving as if he is sitting still. God is already working, but as we come alongside of Him and pray, it moves Him to do great and wonderful things to glorify Himself.

72. What are you asking God to do that can only be explained by His power?

First of all, then, I urge that supplications, prayers, intercessions, and thanksgivings be made for all people... (1 Timothy 2:1)

Much prayer, much power! Little prayer, little power! When we enter into prayer, we are demonstrating faith that God can do more than we could ever do in our own strength.

73. Why do you think it was so important for Paul to entreat Timothy to make much of prayer?

You can use the ACTS method of prayer. This is an acronym for the words Adoration, Confession, Thanksgiving, and Supplication, which includes petition to God for your own needs and intercession to God for one another. Look for scriptures, especially in the Psalms, that would come under these categories that you can pray back to God. Praying God's word is a powerful combination.

Corporate Disciplines

Worship:

But the hour is coming, and is now here, when the true worshipers will worship the Father in spirit and truth, for the Father is seeking such people to worship him. (John 4:23)

> [24] *And let us consider how to stir up one another to love and good works,* [25] *not neglecting to meet together, as is the habit of some, but encouraging one another, and all the more as you see the Day drawing near. (Hebrews 10:24-25)*

> **74. Jesus says worship is not something we just do, but that we are worshipers in the essence of our identity, and we are not to forsake assembling together regularly. Given this, what do you think your commitment to weekly worship should be?**

Community:

> *We know that we have passed out of death into life, because we love the brothers. Whoever does not love abides in death. (1 John 3:14)*

> [42] *And they devoted themselves to the apostles' teaching and the fellowship, to the breaking of bread and the prayers.* [43] *And awe came upon every soul, and many wonders and signs were being done through the apostles.* [44] *And all who believed were together and had all things in common.* [45] *And they were selling their possessions and belongings and distributing the proceeds to all, as any had need.* [46] *And day by day, attending the temple together and breaking bread in*

their homes, they received their food with glad and generous hearts, [47] praising God and having favor with all the people. And the Lord added to their number day by day those who were being saved. (Acts 2:42-47)

The early church not only met weekly for corporate worship, but they also met in small groups in homes for the building of community through personal relationships. They met for prayer, Bible discussion, socially eating together, mutual ministry, worship, and outreach to their un-churched friends.

75. What do you think you can experience in a small group setting that you can't experience in a large worship service?

76. How do you feel about making a commitment to give yourself to the body of Christ through a small group community?

Ministry:

> [11] *And he gave the apostles, the prophets, the evangelists, the shepherds and teachers,* [12] *to equip the saints for the work of ministry, for building up the body of Christ,* [13] *until we all attain to the unity of the faith and of the knowledge of the Son of God, to mature manhood, to the measure of the stature of the fullness of Christ...(Ephesians 4:11-13)*

God has placed each believer in the church and has given each of us gifts to be used in serving Him for the building up of His body. We are not saved *by* service, but we are saved *for* service. God is building a church for His glory. Serving God in His church is the greatest privilege we will ever have. Nothing else even comes close. When we come to the end of our lives, we will have the satisfaction that we had a part in building up of the local church, and in the preparation of the bride of Christ for His coming.

77. How do you believe you can use your gifts, talents, and energy to serve the body of Christ?

Giving:

> [6] *The point is this: whoever sows sparingly will also reap sparingly, and whoever sows bountifully will also reap bountifully.* [7] *Each one must give as he has decided in his heart, not reluctantly or under compulsion, for God loves a cheerful giver. (2 Corinthians 9:6-7)*

"Woe to you, scribes and Pharisees, hypocrites! For you tithe mint and dill and cumin, and have neglected the weightier matters of the law: justice and mercy and faithfulness. These you ought to have done, without neglecting the others. (Matthew 23:23)

[8] Will man rob God? Yet you are robbing me. But you say, 'How have we robbed you?' In your tithes and contributions. [9] You are cursed with a curse, for you are robbing me, the whole nation of you. [10] Bring the full tithe into the storehouse, that there may be food in my house. And thereby put me to the test, says the LORD of hosts, if I will not open the windows of heaven for you and pour down for you a blessing until there is no more need. (Malachi 3:8-10)

God is a giving God. He gave His only son as the most lavish, extravagant gift anyone could give. He has now invited you to participate with Him in his kingdom enterprise of building His church through the giving of our tithes and offerings. In the Bible, every time God challenges us to give financially, He promises great blessings.

Giving is an act of obedience and an act of faith. When we give, we are trusting that God will meet our needs in a much more abundant way than if we had just kept the money and tried to use it to meet our needs ourselves.

The word tithe means tenth. Tithing is a significant Old Testament reference point for us to consider as we purpose in our hearts what God wants us to give. Jesus told the Pharisees that they should practice justice, mercy, and faithfulness without neglecting to continue the practice of tithing. If we are living by grace instead of the law, we should ask God to show us what it would look like to give out of hearts filled with gratitude—for the past grace of God, for the present grace of God, and for the future grace of God.

78. If you are assured that God will bless you abundantly to honor your generous heart, what do you think it means to be a grace giver?

Kingdom Disciplines

Local Outreach:

> [19] *...that is, in Christ God was reconciling the world to himself, not counting their trespasses against them, and entrusting to us the message of reconciliation.* [20] *Therefore, we are ambassadors for Christ, God making his appeal through us. We implore you on behalf of Christ, be reconciled to God. (2 Corinthians 5:19-20)*

You are called to participate with God in His ministry of reconciling people to Himself. The Holy Spirit comes in on the wings of your witness to convict people of sin, to draw them to Jesus, to awaken their hearts to understand and receive the gospel by faith. God wants to use you to share the good news that man is created in His image for the purpose of walking in fellowship with Him. We all were born into sin and separated from God. God solved that problem by sending His son Jesus to die on the cross, paying the penalty for our sins, and offering us a place in heaven. He will give us the gift of eternal life if we receive Him into our lives, trusting in the power of the cross for forgiveness, repenting of our sin, and seeking to follow Him as His disciples in the fellowship and service of His church.

We are called to be witnesses, simply sharing with people what the good Lord has done for us, what our lives were like before we came to Christ, how we came to Christ, and how He has changed us since we came to Him.

> **79.   What if someone came to you and said, "I hear you are a Christian. I am interested in becoming a Christian. Can you tell me what a person needs to do in order to become a Christian?" What would you say to them?**

[37] Then the righteous will answer him, saying, 'Lord, when did we see you hungry and feed you, or thirsty and give you drink? [38] And when did we see you a stranger and welcome you, or naked and clothe you? [39] And when did we see you sick or in prison and visit you? [40] And the King will answer them, 'Truly, I say to you, as you did it to one of the least of these my brothers, you did it to me.' (Matthew 25:37-40)

Jesus had a heart for the poor. He identified with them and tells us that what we do for them we do for Him. There are over 200 references in the Bible that talk about the responsibility of the people of God to meet the needs of the poor.

80.   What would you like to do to meet the needs of the poor in your community?

Global Outreach:

[19] *"Go therefore and make disciples of all nations, baptizing them in the name of the Father and of the Son and of the Holy Spirit,* [20] *teaching them to observe all that I have commanded you. And behold, I am with you always, to the end of the age." (Matthew 28:19-20)*

"Ask of me, and I will make the nations your heritage, and the ends of the earth your possession." (Psalm 2:8)

God is calling all of us to become world Christians with a heart for the world. We may never go as missionaries, but we can all have an investment in God's world mission enterprise by participating in learning, praying, encouraging, supporting, and participating in missions according to God's direction. When we get involved in missions, it expands and broadens our horizons and allows us to get involved in something much bigger than our own little domain.

81. What ways would you like to get involved in what God is doing in the world today?

From your study of the Disciplines of Grace, you can clearly see the beauty of the practice of such disciplines in your life. As you carry out the personal disciplines of Bible study and prayer, the corporate disciplines of worship, community, ministry, and giving, and the kingdom disciplines of local and global outreach, you will see that each plays an important role in your spiritual maturity. As these disciplines become expressions of love because of God's grace, you will flourish and experience your full kingdom potential.

CHAPTER 6

STEP 4 INDUCTIVE BIBLE STUDY METHOD—THE JOURNEY

INTRODUCTION

Our goal is to help guide you to spiritual maturity by offering you a Bible study method that will lead you to a personal word from God each day and help you know what to do with that word when you receive it.

> [15] *Do your best to present yourself to God as one approved, a worker who has no need to be ashamed, rightly handling the word of truth. 2 Tim. 2:15*

Any worthwhile mission involves discipline. Each true disciple-maker commits to disciplines that will improve their ability to listen to and follow Jesus. Devotional Bible study involves learning to listen to God.

INDUCTIVE BIBLE STUDY

Inductive Bible Study involves a deeper study of God that leads to greater understanding, wisdom, and intimacy. This method will lead you to a clear approach to Bible study: Observation, Interpretation, and Application. This Bible study resource will help guide you in the principles of the inductive Bible study method as you study of the life of Christ using the Gospel of Luke.

Devotional Guide

The goal of Bible reading is not information but transformation. It's not about learning facts, but rather knowing God by connecting with Him as He speaks to you through His personal love letter to you. As you begin this plan, do not approach it as a rigid exercise of discipline that you must check off, but rather as an opportunity to get to know the God who created you and who loves you.

You can approach your Bible reading using a process developed by Jerry and Marilyn Fine called "Ponder, Picture, and Pray" [1] As you begin reading, don't be in a hurry. Take your time to ponder the text. As a word or phrase or verse jumps out at you, just underline it and keep on reading. Then come back to each of the underlined verses and read them again, picturing yourself in that geographic setting, and asking God to show you what He wants to say to you personally through that verse. Then pray that verse back to God, personalizing it as you picture the reality of that verse being fulfilled in your life.

This particular plan is a reading of the gospel of Luke. Luke's gospel is the most complete rendering of the life of Christ. The essence of Christianity is that it is a relationship with Jesus Christ, so what better way to develop your relationship with Him than to get to know Him by reading about His life?

Each day as you read, take a minute to pray and ask God to speak to your heart through words, phrases, ideas, or verses that really jump out and grab you. Pray that God's enlightenment will grip your heart with exactly what He wants to say to you. You may want to put a question mark beside the ideas you don't understand. You may want to underline or put a parenthesis around the ideas that grip your heart.

Before you read each day, go back and briefly review the Inductive Bible Study method. Keep it in front of you as you read and fill out the Observation, Interpretation, and Application portions in your daily journal. After you select the specific verses you sense God is speaking to you through, then it can be a powerful experience to write out a prayer to God based upon what you have read.

There is nothing more powerful and intimate than praying God's word back to Him as you personalize it.

As you pray, you can use the ACTS method of prayer, which stands for Adoration, Confession, Thanksgiving, and Supplication. First, acknowledge the attributes of God, for example, that he is all-powerful, all-knowing, omnipresent, merciful, and eternal. Next, confess that you fall short of God's purpose and standards for your life. Third, give thanksgiving for all that He has done for you. Finally, present your petitions and appeals (supplication). The supplication can be divided into petition for your personal needs and intercession for the needs of others. As you pray for your loved ones and their needs, remember that Jesus started the Lord's Prayer with, "Thy kingdom come, thy will be done..." Pray about what God is doing in His wider, larger kingdom. Pray for people you know who do not know Christ, that He would convict them of sin, draw them to Himself, reveal the gospel to them, give them the gift of faith, and even use you to share the gospel with them. Pray for your church and for the missionaries you know. This will expand your vision beyond your own little world to allow you to become a World-Christian and to expand your worldview.

METHOD
Phase I—Observation:

- *Key question – What does it say?*

- **Retell the story. What is the progression of the passage?**

- **Who are the main characters in the passage, and what do you learn about them?**

Phase II—Interpretation:

- *Key question – What does it mean?*

- **What does this passage teach us about God? Man?**

- **What are the primary creative purposes and principles about how to live life God's way?**

Phase III—Application:

- *Key question – How does it apply to my life?*

- **How should I live this out in my life?**

- **How have I fallen short of God's plan? What sins do I need to confess and forsake?**

- **How do I need to trust God to empower me to change through genuine repentance?**

- **How will I be changed if I trust in the death of Christ for forgiveness and inner healing?**

- **What will my life be like if I trust in the presence and power of the Spirit of Christ in me to do what this passage is teaching me?**

Record these each day in a notebook or set up a document on your computer. You will follow a process that will allow you to record what you have discovered in your inductive study. You will then select a key verse that stood out to you; write a journaling prayer to express to God what you are sensing He is calling you to do in applying the truths of that passage to your life.

The following is a template you can follow each day. You will study half a chapter of Luke each day until you finish. When you get together with your mentor, just share with each other what you sensed God was showing you in the scriptures during the past week.

SAMPLE TEMPLATE

Devotional Guide Week One – Day 1

Passage – Luke 1:1-38

 Observation questions, Interpretation questions, and Application questions

The book of Luke will be divided up into the following passages.

Luke 1:1-38, 1:39-80, 2:1-38, 2:39-52, 3:1-20, 3:21-38, 4:1-30, 4:31-44, 5:1-26, 5:27-39, 6:1-23, 6:24-49, 7:1-17, 7:18-50, 8:1-25, 8:26-56, 9:1-26, 9:27-62, 10:1-24, 10:25-42, 11:1-36, 11:37-54, 12:1-34, 12:35-59, 13:1-17, 13:18-35, 14:1-14, 14:15-35, 15:1-10, 15:11-32, 16:1-18, 16:19-31, 17:1-10, 17:11-37, 18:1-17, 18:18-43, 19:1-27, 19:28-48, 20:1-26, 20:27-47, 21:1-24, 21:25-38, 22:1-34, 22:35-71, 23:1-25, 23:26-56, 24:1-12, 24:13-53.

CHAPTER 7

STEP 5 SPIRITUAL PREPARATION

PREPARING FOR THE HARVEST

Jesus Christ is calling you to join him in his ministry of seeking and saving the lost in this world. That is why we call it The Great Commission.

> [19] *"Go therefore and make disciples of all nations, baptizing them in the name of the Father and of the Son and of the Holy Spirit,* [20] *teaching them to observe all that I have commanded you. And behold, I am with you always, to the end of the age." (Matthew 28:19-20)*

This is not a suggestion for professional ministers. It is a command for every follower of Christ.

Before we begin a spiritual journey, we should prepare ourselves spiritually. That begins by considering what motivated Jesus to choose love as his Mission Statement. In Matthew 22:36-40, he was asked,

> *"*[36] *Teacher, which is the great commandment in the Law?"* [37] *And he said to him, "You shall love the Lord your God with all your heart and with all your soul and with all your mind.* [38] *This is the great and first commandment.* [39] *And a second is like it: You shall love your neighbor as yourself.* [40] *On these two commandments depend all the Law and the Prophets."*

Love and compassion will prepare our spirit...

> *35 And Jesus went throughout all the cities and villages, teaching in their synagogues and pro-claiming the gospel of the kingdom and healing every disease and every affliction. 36 When he saw the crowds, he had compassion for them, because they were harassed and helpless, like sheep without a shepherd. 37 Then he said to his disciples, "The harvest is plentiful, but the laborers are few; 38 therefore pray earnestly to the Lord of the harvest to send out laborers into his harvest."* (Matthew 9:35-38)

Compassion for the desperation of our friends compels us to heal, to pray, and to proclaim the good news of how Christ can transform their lives. The compassion of Christ must also break our hearts.

1. According to verse 36, what was it that motivated Jesus to do what He did?

Verse 36 simply says they were "harassed and helpless". But the original word for that is much deeper. It is a word that describes a corpse that has been mangled, a woman who has been ravaged, a person lying prostrate from exhaustion like a drunkard in a gutter, or a soldier lying on the ground with mortal wounds.

2. Who can you think of right now who would fit the images described here?

3. What are they going through?

The desperation of our friends must move us to pray and go.

Imagine a farmer getting up on a clear sunny morning; he walks out and looks out over fields of fully mature wheat, gently swaying in the wind, ready to be harvested. When a farmer has spent all summer plowing and planting and cultivating his crop, and then he sees that the plant is fully grown and ready to be harvested, he gets excited.

4. How should this image make us feel about sharing the good news of the kingdom with others?

As expressed in 1 Thessalonians 1:5, *...because our gospel came to you not only in word, but also in power and in the Holy Spirit and with full conviction. You know what kind of men we proved to be among you for your sake.*

We need to pray for a fresh infilling of the Holy Spirit as we confess our sin and yield every area of our lives to the control of the Holy Spirit so that we will be sterilized scalpels to perform spiritual heart surgery.

This is a suggested prayer to yield all the areas of your life to the control of the Holy Spirit in order to be empowered by Him and to build multiplying disciples of Christ.

Dear Lord Jesus,

Right now, I want to ask you to search my heart and show me if there is any sin for which I need to confess and repent. I confess it to you, trusting in the death of Christ on the cross for forgiveness, healing, and restoration.

I now yield my life to the control of your Spirit.

I yield my mind to your control so that you would be free to place your thoughts into my mind that would allow me to be an effective witness and disciple-maker.

I yield my eyes to your control, that I would be able to see people through the lens of Jesus, that I would have discernment about their needs and how to minister to them.

I yield my ears to your control, that I would always be ready to enter into Spirit-led listening by asking good questions.

I yield my tongue to your control, that I would be ready in season and out of season to initiate spiritual conversations.

I yield my will to your control, that I would always be ready to obey your promptings to speak to people about Christ.

I yield my emotions to your control, that I would have the same compassion and love that Jesus has for those who do not know him.

I yield my body to your control, that I would use my energy to see many people come to know Christ and to be built up into reproducing followers of Christ.

Thank you, that you promised- "if I ask anything according to your will, you will give it to me". I know it is your will that I be filled with your Spirit because you commanded me to receive it. Now, give me the power to walk in the Spirit as I seek to join you in seeing many people become multiplying disciples of Christ.

Amen

CHAPTER 8

STEP 6 INVESTING IN RELATIONSHIPS

When all is said and done, what is really going to matter in your life is not success as the world sees it, but rather who you loved and who loved you. In what relationships are you vested? If disciple-making is viewed as a complex spiritual discipline, that only a few are gifted to accomplish, then it is understandable why we lack confidence in our ability. But, if disciple-making is viewed as loving relationships with a few that can be paid forward and in which God provides the power, then all Christians can participate successfully.

RELATIONAL MINISTRY

The ministry of Jesus was highly relational. When he called the disciples to follow him, he meant to *literally* follow him. He went into the villages and for over three years he carried out a simple method of ministry. He spent time with people socially, he met desperate needs in the lives of people he encountered, and he shared the good news of the kingdom—of what life can be like when it is lived out God's way under God's leadership.

SOCIAL RELATIONSHIPS

⁹ As Jesus passed on from there, he saw a man called Matthew sitting at the tax booth, and he said to him, "Follow me." And he rose and followed him. ¹⁰ And as Jesus reclined at the table in the house, behold, many tax collectors and sinners came and were reclining with Jesus and his disciples. (Matthew 9:9-10)

The first thing Jesus told his new disciple to do was to go back to his house and throw a party. He told him to invite his friends and introduce them to him. The only people Matthew knew were other tax collectors and a group of people who were identified as sinners. This was the plan. His disciples were to reach out to the people in their network of relationships and enjoy their company while introducing them to Jesus.

1.   What are some of the things you like to do and places you like to go to enjoy social relationships?

2.   What if we identified all of the people in our network of relationships and intentionally reached out to just enjoy them and spend time with them socially? This builds trust and creates the environment for entering into spiritual conversations. Does someone come to mind that you need to reach out to more?

MEETING DESPERATE NEEDS

As Jesus went from village to village, he performed miracles by meeting the most desperate needs in the lives of the people he encountered. He healed the sick, raised the dead, fed the hungry, and calmed the raging storm that threatened the lives of his friends. What if we did the same thing? What do you see as the most desperate needs in your community?

What if we regularly pray for the people in our network of relationships and look for desperate needs that we can meet? When our friends are going through a rough time, we can rush like white blood cells to a wound to meet their needs. We will minister to the whole person and earn the right to speak into their lives spiritually.

It could make a huge difference in the quality of our relationships if we are always looking for opportunities to invest in relationships. We can keep a record of birthdays and anniversaries and send cards to celebrate with them. We can look for practical ways to meet the needs of our friends who are hurting.

Once we have made the commitment to invest in relationships that matter, the next step is making a list of friends for whom you will pray. It is extremely important that we write down the names of the people in our network of relationships so that we can keep their names in front of us as we pray for them every day. Go through your contact list and make a list of the names of the different groups of people, and then underline the names of those who do not know Christ.

Immediate Family

Extended Family

Friends

Neighbors

Co-workers

People you do business with

People you used to know

People you would like to know

People in recreational groups

People you meet by divine appointment

CHAPTER 9

STEP 7 PRAYING FOR MY FRIENDS

Jesus taught his disciples to pray. Why? Prayer demonstrates your will to listen and depend upon God's power to lead you to His choice of the person in whose life you are called to invest.

Since so much of the experience of salvation is a work of the Spirit of God, praying for our friends will have a major impact on seeing them come to salvation.

Think of the part that the Holy Spirit plays in a person's salvation. It is the Holy Spirit who convicts us of sin, who draws us to Himself, who takes the blinders off of our eyes so that we can see Christ for who He is, who reveals to us the gospel, who provides kindness that leads us to repentance, who gives us the gift of faith and who breathes the breath of new life into us, causing us to be born again.

There is no more powerful way to pray than to pray according to the Word of God. As you pray, ask God how these verses apply to the people for whom you are praying.

PRAY. . . .

For The Spirit of God to draw them to Himself
"No one can come to me unless the Father who sent me draws him." (John 6:44)

For them to believe the Scriptures
So faith comes from hearing, and hearing through the word of Christ. (Romans 10:17)

That Satan would be prevented from blinding them to the truth
...the god of this world has blinded the minds of the unbelievers, to keep them from seeing the light of the gospel of the glory of Christ, who is the image of God. (2 Corinthians 4:4)

For the Holy Spirit to convict them
[8] "And when he comes, he will convict the world concerning sin and righteousness and judgment..." [13] "When the Spirit of truth comes, he will guide you into all the truth..." (John 16:8,13)

That they would be given the gift of faith.
"Truly, truly, I say to you, whoever hears my word and believes him who sent me has eternal life..." (John 5:24)

That the kindness of God would bring them to repentance.
"Repent therefore, and turn back, that your sins may be blotted out... " (Acts 3:19).

That they would confess Christ as Lord
[9] "...because, if you confess with your mouth that Jesus is Lord and believe in your heart that God raised him from the dead, you will be saved. [10] For with the heart one believes and is justified, and with the mouth one confesses and is saved." (Romans 10:9,10).

That they would take root and grow in Christ
[6] "Therefore, as you received Christ Jesus the Lord, so walk in him, [7] rooted and built up in him and established in the faith, just as you were taught, abounding in thanksgiving." (Colossians 2:6,7).

CHAPTER 10

STEP 8 INITIATING SPIRITUAL CONVERSATIONS

Good questions are always the best way to begin spiritual conversations. The goal of every conversation should be to create "God Space" via a respectful dialog. "God Space" conversations leave people feeling respected and that their opinion matters; this allows God the opportunity to work in them to be open to your point of view.

> *⁵ Walk in wisdom toward outsiders, making the best use of time. ⁶ Let your speech always be gracious, seasoned with salt, so that you may know how you ought to answer each person. (Colossians 4:5-6)*

1. **What do you think it means for your speech to always be "gracious, seasoned with salt"?**

The purpose in a man's heart is like deep water, but a man of understanding will draw it out. (Proverbs 20:5)

2. What do you think is the best way to draw out the deep issues that are in the hearts of people you want to reach?

God gave us two ears and one mouth for a reason. Learn to show genuine interest in people by asking good questions, and you will always have as many friends as you can handle. Good questions serve as a bridge to open up spiritual conversations. Pick one or more that you are most comfortable asking.

- Can I ask your opinion about something? What do you think a church should be doing that really wants to make a difference in their community?
- Do you have an interest in spiritual things?
- Do you have any particular spiritual beliefs?
- What has your faith experience or religious background been like? Was it a positive or negative experience?
- Do you believe in the power of prayer? Is there some way I could pray for you?
- If God could perform a miracle and give you anything you need, what would it be?
- Do you have a desire to grow in your spiritual journey?
- When you hear the word "Christian", what is the first thing that comes to your mind?
- Have you come to a place in your life where you know for sure if you were to die tonight that you would go to heaven, or is that still something you are working out?
- If you were to die tonight and you stood before God and He said, "Why should I invite you into my heaven?", what would you say?
- What do you think a person needs to believe in order to become a Christian?
- Would you be willing to have a Bible discussion about how to gain an assurance of eternal life in heaven and how to experience God's purpose for your life now?

• Can I share with you how I began to experience peace with God?

Now that you have selected one or more questions, role-play asking and responding to one or more with a partner. First, one person asks a question and the other responds; then the reverse.

He has made everything beautiful in its time. Also, he has put eternity into man's heart... (Ecclesiastes 3:11)

3.   How does it affect your confidence to know that God is already working and has set eternity in the heart of each person?

CHAPTER 11

STEP 9 SHARING MY STORY

After we open up a spiritual conversation by asking good questions about their story, we can then transition to sharing our story. A good way to make this transition is to ask, "Can I share with you my God story?" or "Can I share with you how I found peace with God?" Developing a brief, three-minute story will help you avoid a rambling explanation and may always be expanded. The Apostle Paul gave us a beautiful example of how to share our story by the way he shared his story with a high Roman government official. As you read through this account, answer the questions listed in order to begin to craft your own story.

> *¹ So Agrippa said to Paul, "You have permission to speak for yourself." Then Paul stretched out his hand and made his defense: ² I consider myself fortunate that it is before you, King Agrippa, I am going to make my defense today against all the accusations of the Jews, ³ especially because you are familiar with all the customs and controversies of the Jews. Therefore I beg you to listen to me patiently..." (Acts 26:1-3)*

B.C.- MY LIFE BEFORE CHRIST

> *⁴ "My manner of life from my youth, spent from the beginning among my own nation and in Jerusalem, is known by all the Jews. ⁵ They have known for a long time, if they are willing to testify, that according to the strictest party of our religion I have lived as a Pharisee. ⁶ And now I*

stand here on trial because of my hope in the promise made by God to our fathers,[7] to which our twelve tribes hope to attain, as they earnestly worship night and day. And for this hope I am accursed by Jews, O king![8] Why is it thought incredible by any of you that God raises the dead?[9] "I myself was convinced that I ought to do many things in opposing the name of Jesus of Nazareth. [10] And I did so in Jerusalem. I not only locked up many of the saints in prison after receiving authority from the chief priests, but when they were put to death I cast my vote against them.[11] And I punished them often in all the synagogues and tried to make them blaspheme, and in raging fury against them I persecuted them even to foreign cities." (Acts 26:4-11)

1. How would your family and friends have described your life before God showed up in it?

2. What phrase sums up your attitude toward life before you came to know God?

3. What were your greatest struggles and failures?

4. **How did you attempt to meet the needs in your life apart from God?**

5. **Where did you find your sources of identity before you encountered Jesus?**

HOW I ENCOUNTERED CHRIST AND THE GOSPEL

[12] "In this connection I journeyed to Damascus with the authority and commission of the chief priests. [13] At midday, O king, I saw on the way a light from heaven, brighter than the sun, that shone around me and those who journeyed with me. [14] And when we had all fallen to the ground, I heard a voice saying to me in the Hebrew language, 'Saul, Saul, why are you persecuting me? It is hard for you to kick against the goads',

[15] And I said, 'Who are you, Lord?' And the Lord said, 'I am Jesus whom you are persecuting. [16] But rise and stand upon your feet, for I have appeared to you for this purpose, to appoint you as a servant and witness to the things in which you have seen me and to those in which I will appear to you, [17] delivering you from your people and from the Gentiles - to whom I am sending you to open their eyes, so that they may turn from darkness to light and from the power of Satan to God, that they may receive forgiveness of sins and a place among those who are sanctified by faith in me.' (Acts 26: 12-18)

6. Who or what did God use to awaken you to your need for him?

7. What struggles, doubts, and fears did you have about making a commitment to Jesus?

8. When and how did you make a commitment to Jesus? (Be specific)

9. How did you know for sure that a spiritual rebirth had taken place in your life?

10. What kind of "Aha's" do you remember experiencing when you were awakened to the reality of God?

A.D. MY LIFE AFTER RECEIVING CHRIST

19 "Therefore, O King Agrippa, I was not disobedient to the heavenly vision, 20 but declared first to those in Damascus, then in Jerusalem and throughout all the region of Judea, and also to the Gentiles, that they should repent and turn to God, performing deeds in keeping with their repentance. 21 For this reason the Jews seized me in the temple and tried to kill me. 22 To this day I have had the help that comes from God, and so I stand here testifying both to small and great, saying nothing but what the prophets and Moses said would come to pass: 23 that the Christ must suffer and that, by being the first to rise from the dead, he would proclaim light both to our people and to the Gentiles." (Acts 26:19-23)

11. How did God resolve the pain, struggles, and suffering you experienced before receiving Christ?

12.   What changes did God begin to bring about in your attitudes, actions, and appetites?

13.   Were they immediate, or did they take time? Explain.

14.   How is your life different today than it was before you received Christ?

CHAPTER 12

APPENDIX #1

NATURAL DISCIPLESHIP MULTIPLICATION STRATEGY

Each person develops either a One-on-One or a Triad of Spiritual Mentoring with the mentor, a believer, and a person outside the faith.

In each session, you focus on two things according to Jesus' definition of a disciple in Matthew 4:18-20—Following and Fishing. Each session is divided into three parts.

1. Evaluation of last week.
    1. Following- How did you do obeying the teaching from last week?
    2. Fishing- How are you doing in nurturing relationships with people outside the faith?
2. The lesson for the day
3. Plans for following and fishing next week.

If possible, it will be best to develop these spiritual mentoring relationships within your small groups so that the two ministries are not competing with each other but rather complementing each other. If men are mentoring men, women are mentoring women, and teenagers are mentoring their peers, the small groups they are in will be much stronger. Not everyone will be ready to jump in and do this. You will have early adopters, late adopters, and those who will not be ready or able to do it at all. Don't be discouraged; that is just reality. Go with the ones who are ready, and you will still see a great harvest of people come to Christ and built up into multiplying disciples of Christ.

The Pastor will model Natural Evangelism and Discipleship by developing his own track, mentoring the key leader, and being a champion for the cause.

A key leader will oversee the church-wide ministry by providing tracking, accountability, encouragement, and ongoing training.

Tracking can be done with a simple flow chart, listing each team leader and the learner or learners. Appendix 3 includes one you can print out. Then just check the progress as they go along. A template of the flow chart can also be downloaded from www.Naturaldiscipleship.com.

Accountability can be accomplished with one contact a month to each spiritual mentor. This will allow the key leader to connect with them and see how they are doing, providing accountability and guidance for any challenges they are facing. Once the number of mentoring teams exceeds five, the key leader needs to recruit coaching mentors to divide up the calls to the leaders each month. The coaching mentors will report back to the key leader by sending a copy of the updated flow chart and comments. No one person needs to be responsible for more than five mentoring teams.

Ongoing training can be accomplished with one gathering three or four times a year for all those who are involved in spiritual mentoring. This periodic gathering needs to involve a meal, short testimonies of how the spiritual mentoring has changed their lives and a short ongoing training session by the key leader or the pastor. The key leader over the ministry needs to find and develop a man to oversee the men's track, a woman to oversee the women's track and the youth leader to oversee the youth track.

CHAPTER 13

APPENDIX #2

NATURAL DISCIPLESHIP COVENANT

BENEFITS OF A PERSONAL DISCIPLESHIP RELATIONSHIP

There are several reasons why one-to-one or one-to-two discipleship has a unique function that cannot easily be met in a group setting.

1. *More open communication:* If an individual is meeting with another Christian by themselves, they are more willing to be honest in speaking about questions they have or struggles they might be going through. Often, people are hesitant to share personal problems in front of others, but in a one-to-one relationship, they are more likely to talk about the areas in which they really need help. In this way, the discipleship can focus specifically on their particular needs.

2. *Greater accountability:* In a personal relationship, the person being discipled can be held accountable in areas in which they need the most growth. This is an important aspect of Christian development.

3. *Individualized attention:* Personal discipleship allows plenty of time to discuss issues thoroughly and make sure the person being discipled truly understands the concept being discussed; in a group, there may not be enough time to effectively meet individual needs.

4. *Greater intimacy:* A more intimate relationship is much more likely to develop when just two or three people meet together. Deep sharing and growth are much more probable in this type of relationship.

5. *Greater transferability:* A group setting may not effectively equip someone to disciple another believer. With personal discipleship, individuals are trained and equipped to pass on their faith through discipleship, thereby "reproducing reproducers."

Natural Discipleship Covenant

We (Leader) _____ and_____
(Participant) commit to a meeting weekly to build a relationship that creates an atmosphere of community and openness for spiritual growth and understanding of God's Word.

For this to become a reality, we commit to these simple steps of accountability:

1. Be committed to being on time and at every session (unless there is a family emergency or other uncontrollable event).
2. Be prepared by reading through and answering all the questions in the materials.
3. Be willing to be transparent, authentic, and confidential with one another.
4. Be willing to transfer what you have learned to someone else in a new discipling relationship.

CHAPTER 14

APPENDIX #3

NATURAL DISCIPLESHIP PROGRESS CHART

We have created a template of a progress chart for you. You can print the spreadsheet shown on the next two pages to keep track of your progress through the lessons. The progress chart is also available at Naturaldiscipleship.com if you would like to monitor your progress electronically. Simply download it and use it as an Excel spreadsheet and note completion of each section.

Natural Discipleship Progress Chart

Participants/ Sessions		Discipler	Disciple 1	Disciple 2
Name				
Phone				
Email				
Spiritual Preparation				

Investing in Relationships				
Praying for My Friends				
Initiating Spiritual Conversations				
Sharing My Story				
Sharing His Story				
Life's Most Important Questions Sessions	1			
	2			
	3			
	4			

Natural Discipleship Progress Chart Page 2

Sessions Continued		Discipler	Disciple 1	Disciple 2
Name				

Groundwork Series Sessions	1			
	2			
	3			
	4			
	5			
	6			
The Journey Session Weeks	1			
	2			
	3			
	4			
	5			
	6			
	7			
	8			

1.   From One on One with God, by Jerry & Marilyn Fine. Copyright 2003, www.OneonOnewithGod.org. Used by permission. ↑

Experience Even More

Natural Discipleship

provides an app that offers the tools and resources needed to help people have a personal multiplication discipleship ministry.

Download The App

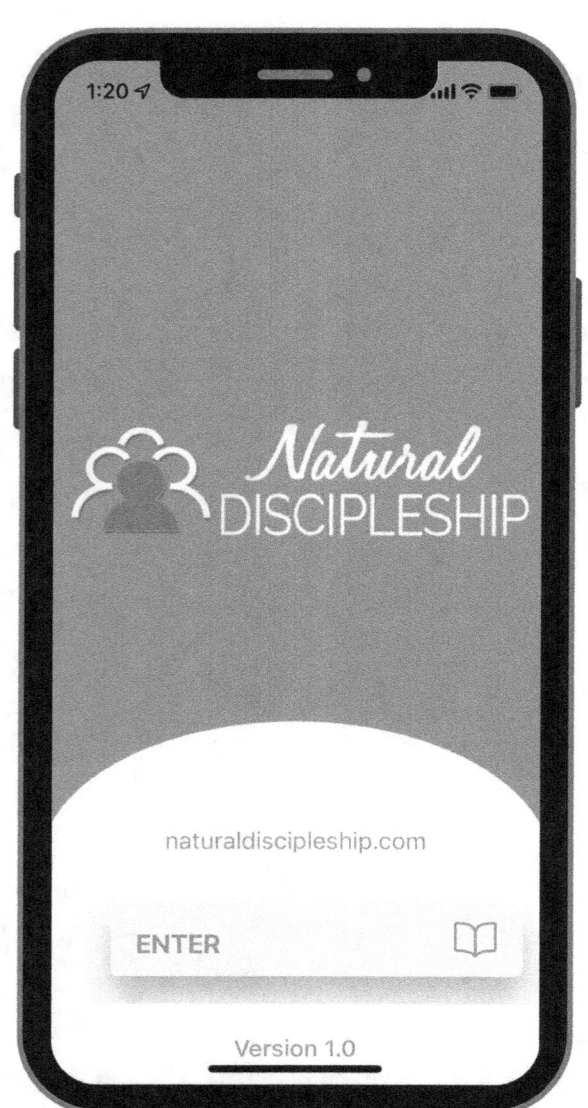

Experience Even More

Natural DISCIPLESHIP
a Be Mission Minded Ministry

Natural Discipleship offers four curriculum resources that are essential in assisting you with your personal discipleship ministry focused on multiplication.

- The 9-Step Multiplication
- The Discover the Keys to Being Set Free
- The 5 Keys to Building a Leadership team
- The 5 Keys to leading a Spiritual Movement

Start your personal discipleship ministry focused on multiplication today!

www.naturaldiscipleship.com